Ovaltineys to Sheredean Girls Club 1941 to 1960

~

MICHAEL PARKINSON (THE OTHER ONE)

Published by Michael Parkinson
Publishing partner: Paragon Publishing, Rothersthorpe
First published 2019
© Michael Parkinson, 2019

ISBN 978-1-78222-675-8

Book design, layout and production management by Into Print
www.intoprint.net
+44 (0)1604 832149

Foreword by Editor Jenny Green

Having read Michael's first book "from Billy Fury to You Tube", in which he uniquely has over 200 You Tube titles to accompany and enhance the text, my interest was piqued when he told me he was embarking on a second project. What would this entail?

For those of us of a certain age Michael's latest book "Ovaltineys to Sheredean Girls' Club 1941 - 1960" is a glorious trip down Memory Lane.

For the younger generation it gives an insight of growing up in a 'freer' society and may well give rise to comments such as "Did children my age do those kinds of things?" or "Did my Nan really do that?"

For all generations however, it illustrates the strength and longevity of the bonds which shared activities can forge.

A thoroughly good read.

JRG

Comment by Michael Parkinson

What Jenny is too modest to mention is that she edited my first book and not only refused to accept any payment but insisted on buying a copy of the published work at the full price.

She has not had so much work to do on this book because I decided that chapters 2 to 15 would be printed exactly as the girls had written, warts and all. Jenny has only needed to edit the remaining chapters that were written by me.

MP

Contents

Explanation of local terms;-

An Iced Lolly is known in the Nottingham Area as a 'Sucker'
Lambley Dumbles is an area of woodland situated close to the village of Lambley in Nottinghamshire. It is situated about 4 miles from Arnold where the Sheredean Club was based.

Acknowledgements

- Arnold Local History Group for extended loan of the Sheredean Log Books
- Kings Langley Local History and Museum Society for information about the Ovaltine factory
- Associated British Foods and Twinings for permission to use the Ovaltine story
- Wander AG, Neuenegg, Switzerland for information about Ovaltine
- Hertfordshire County Council Library Service
- Barnardo's, for permission to use the Princess Diana picture
- Jenny Green, for editing and advice
- My wife, Joan Parkinson for all the proof reading and perseverance
- Renewable Energy Solutions for information about the Ovaltine Egg Farm
- Mark Webb at Paragon Publishing, Rothersthorpe who are the publishers of this book
- Mrs Pat Briggs (Stacey) for the constant supply of information by letter and telephone
- Surviving members of the Sheredean Club for messages and information
- Youth Hostel Association for permission to use information from their web site.
- Eric Miller and David Gibbins for converting the slide to picture format
- To all the people who have helped in any way

Chapter 1 Introduction

Written by Michael Parkinson

ALFRED STACEY MARRIED DORIS ON 19 April 1930. As youngsters Alf had been in the Boy Scouts and Doris in the Girls Brigade they first met whilst both were camping at Shere in Sussex so shared their interest in camping and the out door life. Prior to their marriage Alf was living in London and worked as a commercial traveller selling meat and frozen goods. Doris was living in Camden Terrace, Brighton and worked at the Lyon and Hall music shop on East Street in the town.

When they were married Alf was asked to work the midlands area and the couple lived in a rented house on George St in Arnold which is situated four miles north of Nottingham.

Pat, their first daughter was born in hospital at Nottingham on 29 October 1933.

Shortly afterwards the family moved to a rented cottage in Keyworth, about six miles south of Nottingham. After a few years the family moved into another rented house at 66 Sandfield Road in Arnold. The house was owned by a lady named Mrs Mee who lived next door, she kept bees and Pat used to go round and help her to 'Spin the Honey'. Mr and Mrs Reed lived next door, on the other side, they had no children so gave their sweet ration coupons to Pat's family. Pat's Father, Alf Stacey was an 'Air Raid Precaution Warden' and the Stacey house was the local ARP post. Pat remembers that there were sandbags outside the window. Alf used to car share with a Mr Gwilliam from West Bridgford to make the petrol ration coupons go a bit further.

Pat told me that they had a very long garden and 'one morning I woke up to see two large horses on the lawn, I went in to tell my parents, they didn't believe me but later my father helped to get them back to the farm, 3 doors away'. She told me that she used to watch the 'lamp lighter' come along in the evening to put the gas light on outside the house, and off again in the morning. She had (and still has) an old His Masters Voice wind up record player, her first records were 'The Teddy Bears Picnic' and 'Pinocchio'. They also had dance records and would push back the chairs and dance around in the lounge.

Alf was doing well in his job and had a company car which he was allowed to use for personal as well as business use. The family got on well with Mrs Mee and Alf negotiated a deal with her for the purchase of the previously rented house so they became owners of 66 Sandfield Road. (The numbers of the houses on Sandfield Road were changed many years later so 66 is not the number of the Stacey house as I write in 2019 MP). The house had a very large back garden which became even bigger because Alf bought an adjoining piece of land at the end. They decided to give the house a name 'Sheredean'. Shere in Sussex was where they had met and dean was included because Doris and Alf had done much of their courting around Roeden, Rottingdean and Saltdean which are just along the coast from Brighton where Doris lived.

When Pat was five years old she went to Daybrook School in Arnold and transferred to Arno Vale Infants School which is situated in Woodthorpe (the neighbouring parish) in 1943, and was there for one year. I and my two sisters were later to attend the same school which is still there as I write in 2019 with the name Woodthorpe Infant School. On leaving Arno Vale Pat went on to Arnold Church Drive Senior Girls Council School just before her 11th birthday. The head teacher was Miss E.W.Temple. Pat was form Vice Captain in year 44 to 45, and house Captain 45 to 46. Her memories of that school were doing weaving in the first year, gardening in year two and 'make do and mend' in year three. She had to stay at school until age 15 because the leaving age had just been changed from 14. Another daughter, Wendy, was born on 19 November 1939.

When Pat was 8 years old Eileen Foster was one of her friends, Eileen's parents ran a market garden business and so occupied a farmhouse and a large plot of land on the opposite side of Sandfield Road to Pat. The two girls and some friends joined 'The League of Ovaltineys' and met in the Hay Loft at the Fosters cottage to listen to the Ovaltineys programme on Radio Luxembourg. The Horse and Cart that Mr Foster used to take his produce to market was situated underneath the Hay Loft and the group of girls went into the parlour where Mrs Foster played piano and taught the girls to sing 'We are the Ovaltineys'. This song was used at the start of all the radio programmes which were sponsored by the makers of Ovaltine a popular night time drink. Pat has loaned me her personalised copy of the official rule book from 'The League of Ovaltineys'. Here are the words of the song that opened the programmes:-

We are the Ovaltineys, little girls and boys
Make your requests, we'll not refuse you
We are here just to amuse you
Would you like a song or story?
Will you share our joys?
At games and sports we're more than keen
No merrier children could be seen
Because we all drink Ovaltine
We're happy girls and boys.

Certification that Pat was a member of the League of Ovaltineys

I have received permission to include my story about Ovaltine and the Ovaltineys, it will feature as chapter 18 of this book and will include all 12 pages of the League of Ovaltineys Rule Book.

I asked José if she could remember being in the Hay Loft at the Market Garden and this is her reply

Hi Michael,

I did indeed listen to the Ovaltineys as a child, I did know Eileen and her brother Ralph. I remember the market garden business well, remember having to wait for Eileen to do her piano practice before she could come out to play. I remember playing in the Hay Loft as well but don't remember listening to the Ovaltineys whilst in the loft although I could well have done. Remember being fascinated when I saw a big bath of tied 'bunches' of radishes being washed by a hose fed into a big galvanised bath. Also Mr Foster and his carts (there were often two carts, each with a horse at the front passing our house at about 3 a.m. in the morning on the way to market). I am sure that is how we came to use the Ovaltineys idea of an introductory and closing chorus at our concerts.

Best Wishes José

Pat recalls that she and her friends used to play in the Air Raid Shelter or Rhubarb House (a dark old cottage which was situated next to Fosters Cottage). She recalled that she and her friends would take some sugar on a saucer down the Market Garden land and sit in the hedgerow whilst eating rhubarb dipped in sugar.

Soon afterwards Pat's Father wrote a story especially for her which he called 'Pat finds the fairies'. Many years later Pat's son, Michael added illustrations to the story and got six copies printed, just for family members. Michael is considering publishing this as a children's book.

Alf changed his job and starting selling crockery and cooking utensils. In his spare time he did some acting and performed as 'Master of Ceremonies' for 'Holidays at Home' and 'Children on Shire Horses' in Arnold Park which I have been told, he organised. He was also MC at sporting and social events including the sports day at his daughters' school. Pat told me that at school she was known as 'the girl with the father on the mike'.

In May 2018 my first book titled 'From Billy Fury to YouTube' was published. One of the chapters was called 'Childhood Memories' and this is a paragraph that I included:-

My sisters had a friend called Pat Stacey who set up a club for her friends which she called 'The Sheredean Club' she organised little concerts and plays in the family back garden and persuaded her father to provide music. After a few years they got ambitious and organised a show in the hall of Front Street Baptist Church at Arnold, I was asked to operate the curtains, one rope to open and another one to close, so I had to stand at the side of the stage. One of the routines was South Sea Island dancing for which dad had provided the raffia for the grass skirts. I really enjoyed the show and my close up view of the dancing girls. A full account of the Sheredean club is in the Arnold Library.

On 2 July 2018 I went into the Arnold library and asked to see the book about the Sheredean Club, a man named Ralph Lloyd-Jones searched through all the relevant records and could find no trace of the book or of it having ever being given to them. Ralph was extra diligent in his search because if the book was given to Arnold library he would have been responsible for making sure that it was available. The following day I contacted my elder sister who had given me the information about the book being in Arnold library and she insisted that it should be there. She put me in touch with Pat Stacey (now Pat Briggs an 85 year old lady living in Somerset) Pat insisted that in June 2016 she had donated the books, (two of them) to the Arnold library and that they should be there. She gave me the telephone number and name of the man who she had given them to. When I contacted the man it transpired that he was the chairman of Arnold Local History Group and the books were safely deposited in their archives. I was told that if Pat gave permission to the secretary of the history group the books could be loaned to me. Pat and the secretary liaised by telephone and I made arrangements to collect the books.

When I examined the books I was impressed and excited with what was revealed. Here was a story of a twelve year old girl who had started and organised a club for girls in 1945, the year that the second world war finished and Britain was in the grip of austerity. Pat called them Log Books and it was obvious that she had shown management skills well beyond her tender years because she had persuaded club members, some as young as eight years of age, to write essays on some of the club activities. I felt privileged to turn the pages and read what was before me. It was sometimes an emotional experience to read some of the contents of the books. This was all achieved before computers, spell checkers, and other writing aids that we take for granted in 2019. In fact when they started to use a typewriter a few years later the results were mediocre to say the least.

The front of the first log book, a bit grubby but it has been handled for nearly 60 years

I decided to share the contents of the books on YouTube and spent all my spare time for eight weeks in narrating the story whilst videoing the hand written text so the result is like an audio book. This, in my opinion, was very important because there were some spelling mistakes or grammatical errors and I decided it was up to the readers to determine what was correct or incorrect. The YouTube title relevant to this chapter is:-

Sheredean Girls Story Introduction Audio and text

The story emerged that from 1945 to 1960 of a group of girls taking part in varied club activities. They grew salad plants and sold them to raise funds, they went hiking, camping, put shows on with poetry, song and dance, went Carol singing at Christmas and donated funds to Dr Barnardo's Homes. They made handcrafted items and sold them at their concerts to raise money. They ran the club on democratic terms, held meetings, sometimes by torchlight, in the shed of Pat's parents garden. Both my sisters were in the club at various times and they have told me that the emphasis was on having fun and enjoyment as they involved themselves in all the activities.

I have been in contact with José, a former member of the club who has written *'Dear Michael, I was pleased to receive your letter and have managed to view and listen to some of the story on YouTube. I think it is a lovely idea that you have had and am interested in your book, is it the printed account of our Sheredean Club? If so I would very much like to buy a copy. My family are very interested to keep and read it. (I love the way you have presented it on YouTube, just as it was written, mistakes and all-wonderful, thank you.) Reading some of the story you cannot but notice the "freedom" we had whilst we were growing up as opposed to the way children live now. As you will realise I was involved mainly in the early days, which was before my dancing took over and I went away dancing in Pantomime. But I so much remember camping at the end of Stacey's very long garden, and once we had packed up and decamped down there were not allowed to come back to the house except to use the outside toilet. The rule was "if you had forgotten something you will have to make do without it" just as you would have to do if camping away from home. I remember making a steamed pudding which was very successful and light having been made in one of the "billycans". I also remember us having our meetings in a garden shed also at the bottom of Stacey's garden and apart from torches, we used candles as lights.We were forever knitting and sewing and selling what we had made to raise money for Dr Barnardo's. Strangely enough I am still involved in craft and fundraising and even now am doing the same sort of thing with our local Women's Institute.*

Very best wishes, José

Decimalisation of the British monetary system took place in 1971 so for the benefit of younger readers I explain the system used during the writing of this book.

The basic system was made up of :-

Pounds, symbol, £ - Shillings, symbol s - Pennies, symbol d - Example £2 12s 4d

The penny had lower value coins, Farthings and Halfpennies, Two farthings in a halfpenny and two halfpennies in one penny.

There were 12 pennies d in one shilling s

20 shillings in one £ so a pound was worth 240 pennies

Further coins were threepenny pieces (worth 3d)

Sixpenny pieces worth sixd

Two shilling pieces worth 24d

Half crowns worth 30d or 2s and 6d

There were ten shilling notes, worth ten s and pound notes worth twenty s

Five pound notes were worth five £

The symbols were often not included so for example £6 14 shillings ten pence and 3 farthings would be printed as £6-14-10¾

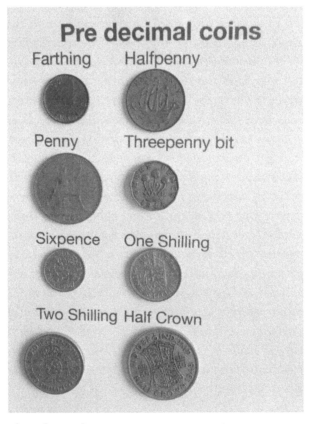

An example of pre decimalisation coins

Sheredean Chapter 2

1945 to 1947
Written by Pat Stacey with essays by Rosemary Lockley and Janet Morris

THE SHEREDEAN STORY LOGBOOK WAS written by Pat Stacey (who was 12 years old in 1945), Pat organised members of the club to write essays into the book as things progressed, the first page started like this MP):- This club was first started (1945) and as this log book has only just been started in 1951 we can only put in a bit about the past years.

When we first started we called ourselves the 'Avonlea Club' and our meetings were held at Rosemary's house (named Avonlea at 101 Sandfield Road). Other members of the club were Eileen and Mor. Here I will ask Rosemary to put in what she remembers of our first Pantomime.

In the summer of 1945, the club put on a pantomime. We called it 'Dick Whittington. The characters were as follows:-
Dick - Morfydd Price
Alice - Eileen Foster
Puss - John Price (John was presumably Morfydd's Brother MP)
Merchant - Pat Stacey
Cook - Rosemary Lockley

The Pantomime was in three acts with an interval between each. The first scene was in the Kitchen of the Merchant's house, the second on the roadside, the third was the wedding day. I had written the script and we put some songs into it. We acted the pantomime in our garden before an invited audience. It had rained during the day, making the afternoon impossible but the evening was fine and warm.

Before the show, we had all gone to friends houses to show off our costumes. The evening was a great success and everyone thoroughly enjoyed it.

Rosemary Lockley

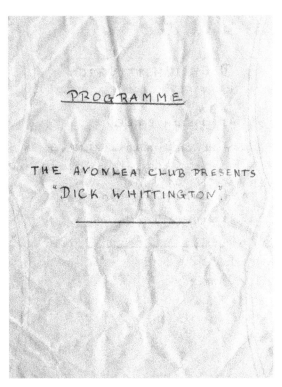

The front of the first hand made programme

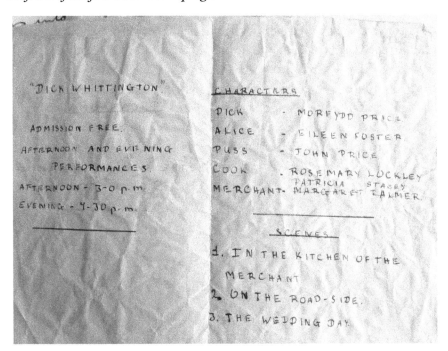

The inside of the programme

Later this club fell through, I can't just remember why, but it did. I restarted it in 1946 over here at Sheredean so we named it the Sheredean Club. We held it in the shed on Thursday evenings. Members were Eileen, Rosemary, Mor, José, and later Ann. Amongst other things we had a piece of garden on which we grew vegetables and sold them to our friends. The club made 2s-3d which we put in our club funds. Here I must say that each member tries to bring 1d each week to put into the box, for during the winter we have torches in the shed, so we have to have some money to buy the batteries for them, also money for seeds etc.

After this club had been started the younger ones wanted a club, so I began a Junior Club, (in 1947) which we held on Tuesday evenings, to which came Janet, Gillian and Wendy. Here I think Janet will put in a bit about our first junior club concert.

Our first concert was held on June 17th 1947. It was performed by the Junior Club on a Tuesday night in the Club's garden. We invited the Senior Club and our parents.

Pianoforte solos were given by Wendy, Pat and me. In the middle of her piece Wendy made a mistake and shouted 'dash it' which caused fun for everyone.

Singing by Pat, Gillian and me was followed by a dance from Gillian.

We all said a piece of poetry. Wendy and I brought the concert to an end with a small dialogue entitled:-'In the Garden' Wendy was the Snowdrop and I was the Crocus.

Janet Morris

We were all well pleased with the results of the concert so we decided to have one the following year. By this time we had lost Gillian and Mor and gained Margaret and Joyce.

This year we had competitions for the Best Attendance and highest points. Senior Club points were won by Ann with 72 points and Junior Club points by Janet with 125 points. Senior Club Attendance was a draw between Ann and José with 13 out of a possible 22. Junior Club, Wendy with 27 out of 27. At the end of the year prizes were given to these girls. The gardening results were better this year. Senior Club made 7s-7d and Junior Club 7s-4d which again went into club funds. I arranged a Carol singing party and we raised the sum of 13s-6d for Dr Barnardo's Homes.

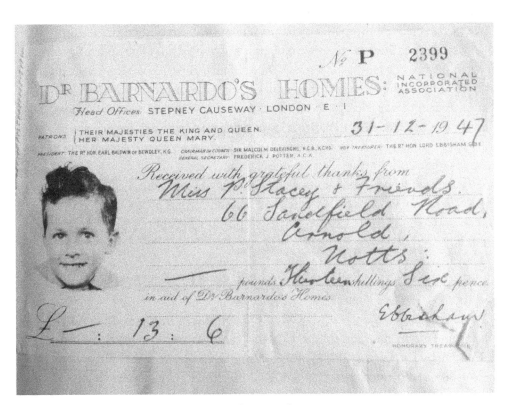

The first receipt from Dr Barnardo's for 13/6d

Sheredean Chapter 3

1948

Written by Pat Stacey, essays by Ann Parkinson and José Packwood

IN 1948 WE DECIDED WE would join the clubs together for the concert. The play I wanted to do was 'The Woodcutter' but this couldn't be done as Margaret could not get to practices because of homework.

This year we had decided to try to make a little money on the concert but as the admission was only 2d had to think of something else to make money. So we decided on having a sale of work. We all got busy and very soon had quite a nice collection of small articles. Here I will hand over to Ann and let her write about the concert.

The first joint club concert was held in 1948. The opening chorus was composed by José and it has been used in each concert since. The main point of the concert was the play which was written by Mr Stacey. It was called 'The breakfast fairies' José played the part of a very good natured mother and Janet and myself played the part of her two daughters, Wendy and Marie. Wendy played the part of Fairy good voice and Gillian was her rival, Nasty, the evil voice. José did two solo dances and with Gillian and Wendy danced the acrobatic dance called 'The Slave Dance'. Janet recited 'All the way to Alfriston'. Pat sang the 'Clappy Song' and Janet sang the 'Cradle Song'. José amused us by saying the 'Sultan and the Sultana'. Joyce said a little poem called 'Snowdrops' and sang 'My Bed is like a little Boat'.

Ann Parkinson

(I can't remember this song but have discovered that the words were written by Robert Louis Stevenson and include the poem here MP)

My bed is like a little boat;
Nurse helps me in when I embark;
She girds me in my sailor's coat
And starts me in the dark.

At night I go on board and say
Good-night to all my friends on shore;
I shut my eyes and sail away
And see and hear no more.

19

And sometimes things to bed I take,
As prudent sailors have to do;
Perhaps a slice of wedding-cake,
Perhaps a toy or two.

All night across the dark we steer;
But when the day returns at last,
Safe in my room beside the pier,
I find my vessel fast.

Robert Louis Stevenson

And here José will write in the Chorus.
Opening Chorus:-
This is the club from Sheredean to greet you with a smile
For you have to wear a smile these days to make your life worth while,
We'll try to entertain you, and please you too you know,
"So-oo!" we are the Sheredeaners hoping that you like our show.

Ending Chorus
The club is bidding goodbye to you all with a smile,
For you have to wear a smile these days to make your life worth while
We've tried to entertain you, and please you too you know,
"So-oo!" we are the Sheredeaners hoping that you liked our show.

José Packwood

[I sent a message to José asking what tune was used for the song and here is the reply MP]

Hi Michael – Had to "sing it to myself" to remember it's to "Pack up your troubles in your old kitbag and smile smile smile," which is where I must have pinched "for you have to wear a smile these days to make you life worthwhile" This of course was around a lot from the war etc. I had a little laugh to myself as I remembered we used to almost shout out the "So-oo!" before singing the "we are the Sheredeaners" etc

You are certainly jogging my memory. If you can't remember the tune yourself (you are younger than us) ask Ann to sing it to you.

Best wishes José

(How could José think I did not know this song, it is one of my favourite childhood memories MP) The concert was again a great success and we made £1-10s which we donated to Dr Barnardo's Homes.

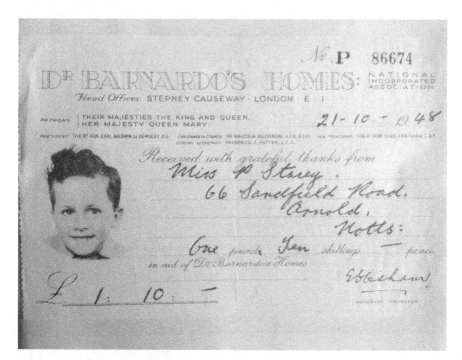

Receipt from Dr Barnardo's for £1-10 shillings

Club Concert 1948

Club Play 1948

Wendy as a fairy, 8 years

José as a dancer, 14 years

During this year the Junior Club read Peter Pan, which they all enjoyed very much. We also had a silver paper collection and we were thanked in the Nottingham Evening Post by Tinker Bell.

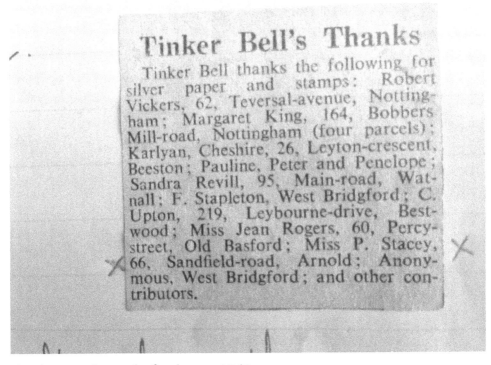

Tinker Bell's Thanks

Tinker Bell thanks the following for silver paper and stamps: Robert Vickers, 62, Teversal-avenue, Nottingham; Margaret King, 164, Bobbers Mill-road, Nottingham (four parcels); Karlyan, Cheshire, 26, Leyton-crescent, Beeston; Pauline, Peter and Penelope; Sandra Revill, 95, Main-road, Watnall; F. Stapleton, West Bridgford; C. Upton, 219, Leybourne-drive, Bestwood; Miss Jean Rogers, 60, Percy-street, Old Basford; Miss P. Stacey, 66, Sandfield-road, Arnold; Anonymous, West Bridgford; and other contributors.

Now here are the results for the year 1948.

Senior Club, attendance. Ann 36 out of a possible 44.

Points Ann with 261.

Money, José who had brought 4s 11d during the year.

Junior Club, attendance. Wendy 42 out of 46.

Points Janet with 331.

Money, Wendy with 9s 2d.

These girls also received small prizes such as books, writing pads and diaries.

The gardening results were Senior Club 7s 2d, Junior Club 3s 7d.

Again we went Carol singing and this time we collected £1-2s for Dr Barnardo's Homes.

During this year (Oct 6th) we went to the Bonington Cinema in Arnold to see Bambi, which we all enjoyed very much. The club and members shared the cost of the outing.

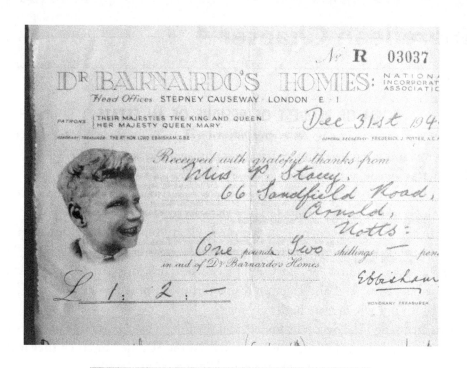

Dr Barnardo's Homes

№ R 03037

Head Offices STEPNEY CAUSEWAY · LONDON · E · 1

PATRONS | THEIR MAJESTIES THE KING AND QUEEN
HER MAJESTY QUEEN MARY

Dec 31st 194-

Received with grateful thanks from
Miss P. Stacey,
66 Sandfield Road,
Arnold,
Notts:
One pound Two shillings — pen
in aid of Dr Barnardo's Homes

£1 : 2 : —

DR. BARNARDO'S HOMES

NATIONAL INCORPORATED ASSOCIATION

Patrons { THEIR MAJESTIES THE KING AND QUEEN
HER MAJESTY QUEEN MARY

BARNARDO-DAY FUND

Chairman : BRYAN E. FICCIS, Esq.
Secretary : ANEURIN JONES, B.A.

Telegrams : JONES, WAIFDOM, EDO, LONDON
Telephone : STEPNEY GREEN 3400
Head Office : 18-26, STEPNEY CAUSEWAY,
LONDON, E.1.

IC

14th January, 1949.

Miss P. Stacey,
66, Sandfield Road,
Arnold,
Notts.

Dear Miss Stacey,

It is with warm appreciation I acknowledge
the welcome gift of 15/-d., being the result of a
Carol Singing effort made by you and your friends,
also for the Christmas Tree gift of 7/-d. I should
be grateful if you would convey to your fellow
Carollers my warmest thanks.

Were it possible for you to see the
expressions of joy on the faces of our boys and
girls on a Christmas morning they would indeed
convey our gratitude to you more effectively than
any written words of thanks.

Our large family of more than 7,000 boys
and girls send greetings and best wishes to you all.

Yours sincerely,

Aneurin Jones

Pat received this nice letter from Dr Barnardo's

Sheredean Chapter 4

1949
Written by Pat Stacey, essay by Joy McRobert

IN 1949 WE OFFICIALLY JOINED the clubs together. Unfortunately Margaret had not been coming regularly, but started coming again in July. Here I will ask Joy McRoberts to write in about our sale of work and concert of 1949.

The concert of 1949 was the first one I had ever seen and after seeing how everybody enjoyed themselves I decided to join the Sheredean Club.

The first item was a poem by Jean Sumpton called "A little mistake" and then we had another poem by Janet Morris this was called 'The Raggle Taggle Gypsy's'. We then had a poem read by Pat, our Captain, called "The Cosy Cottage" which was composed by Ann. And also Captain read a poem composed by herself called "A Spring Morning" which were both very nice.

Ann then sang "The Second Minuet" and then there were two more poems, one by Wendy called "Porridge" and then by Joyce "At the Seaside" and then they had a play (written by Mr Stacey) which was called 'White Magic', with:-

Wendy	-	Janie
Janet	-	Hilda
Ann	-	Mrs Plum
José	-	Miss Flapper
Captain	-	Brown Owl
Gillian	-	Flower Girl
Joyce	-	Passer by

Then they had one or two more poems and then a dance by Wendy and Gillian called the Slave Dance. José then danced the Polish Mazurka. Captain sang On Wings of Song and then José gave a Puppet Show.

Everything was very enjoyable and the evening was a great success.

Joy McRobert

This year the concert was better than ever and we made about £4 which we put into club funds. Our audience of about 40 were all well pleased and applauded each item very well. Just before the concert we had a new member who was enrolled after the concert along with a second new member (Joy McRobert and Jean Sumpton). At the end of the year we lost Joyce Parkinson as the family moved further away and it was a long way for her to come she being only 8 years old.

Our next excitement was the making of the guy which Margaret and I did between us, it was very life like and made some of the young children cry as they thought he was a real man. On Guy Fawkes night we had a marvellous time round the bonfire, singing, eating and letting off fireworks.

This year we sent two parcels off to Tinker Bell, here are the cuttings from the paper.

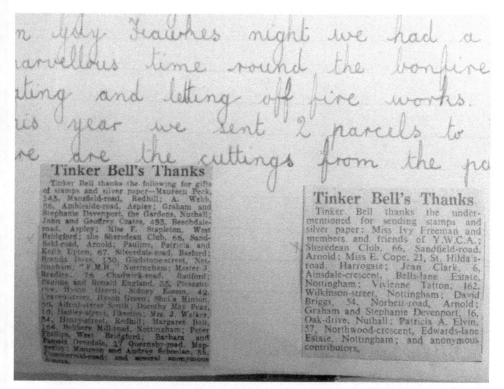

As we had not sent our concert money to Dr Barnardo's we decided to we would make Christmas Stockings and send these which we did along 4-/3½ with some other things, including 1-10½ worth of farthings. (At four to a penny I calculate that was 90 farthings MP)

FJP/BH/AW

HEAD OFFICES:

Stepney Causeway,
London, E.1.

15th December, 1949

Miss Pat Stacey,
66, Sandfield Road,
Arnold, Notts.

My dear Pat,

We have been so pleased to receive your letter and the very welcome remittance of 4/3½d which you have been good enough to send towards our Christmas Tree collection and for which I enclose the official receipt with our Honorary Treasurer's very warmest thanks.

We are also very glad to have the nice Christmas parcel which you have sent for the benefit of our children from the members of the Sheredean Club, and I should be grateful if you would convey to them all an expression of our sincere gratitude for their generosity. I can assure you that the contents will be much appreciated by some of our little folk and I enclose the official receipt herewith.

With many thanks again and with every good wish to you all for Christmas and the New Year,

Yours sincerely,

General Secretary.

Another thank you letter and receipt from Dr Barnardo's.

28

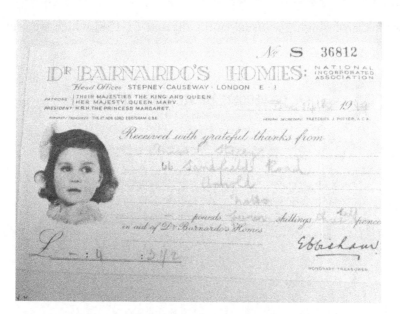

Dr BARNARDO'S HOMES: NATIONAL INCORPORATED ASSOCIATION

Head Offices STEPNEY CAUSEWAY · LONDON · E · 1

PATRONS | THEIR MAJESTIES THE KING AND QUEEN
HER MAJESTY QUEEN MARY.
PRESIDENT H.R.H. THE PRINCESS MARGARET.

№ S 36812

Received with grateful thanks from

in aid of Dr Barnardo's Homes

DR. BARNARDO'S HOMES

NATIONAL INCORPORATED ASSOCIATION.

Patrons | THEIR MAJESTIES THE KING AND QUEEN
HER MAJESTY QUEEN MARY.

All Communications should be addressed to the Head Offices.
18 to 36, STEPNEY CAUSEWAY, LONDON, E.1.

T 17955   Dec 13th 1949

Received with grateful thanks from

Miss P. Stacey

Gift of

3 Picture Books
1 Xmas Stockings
2 Stamp Collecting Outfits
1 Xylophone
1 Game & Xmas Cards
1 Jigsaw
2 Washer Pencils
1 Bead Necklace
3 Prism Toys
2 Purses
2 Leather Cases
1 Painting Outfit
1 Tooth Brush

P T Kirkpatrick

General Superintendent

We went Carol Singing as usual, and collected £1-15-0 which we sent to Dr Barnardo's.

DR. BARNARDO'S HOMES

NATIONAL INCORPORATED ASSOCIATION

Patrons { THEIR MAJESTIES THE KING AND QUEEN
{ HER MAJESTY QUEEN MARY

President: HER ROYAL HIGHNESS THE PRINCESS MARGARET

ARNARDO-DAY FUND

Chairman: BRYAN E. FIGGIS, Esq.
Secretary: ANEURIN JONES, B.A.

GL.

Telegrams: JONES, WAIFDOM, EDO, LONDON
Telephone: STEPNEY GREEN 3400

Head Office: 18-26, STEPNEY CAUSEWAY,
LONDON, E.1.

10th January 1950.

Miss P. Stacey,
66, Sandfield Road,
Sheredean,
Arnold.

Dear Miss Stacey,

I should like you to know how deeply we appreciate your generous gift of £1.15s.0d. as a result of a Carol Singing effort by members of the Sheredean Club.

Our post at this time of the year is abnormally heavy, and for this reason you will appreciate that we are unable to deal with correspondence as promptly as we would wish.

Through the continued help of our friends we are privileged to replace memories of loneliness, neglect, need and insecurity so often the sad lot of many who pass through our Ever Open Door, by the companionship, care and love which has always characterized these Homes.

We are most grateful to all concerned for their kindness in giving thought to our large family of boys and girls, many of whom have spent their first Christmas in our midst.

Thank you very much,

Yours sincerely,

Aneurin Jones

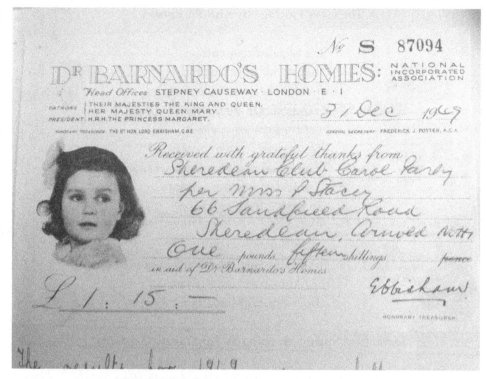

The results for 1949 are as follows,

Attendance, Wendy with 28 out of 34. Money, José with 2/9½. Points, Ann with 283 who beat Janet by one point. The gardening result was 9/6.

The year was well finished off with a Christmas party, at which Wendy, José and Ann received their prizes. We invited Mummy and Daddy and Ann, being our Club Leader, gave Mummy and Daddy a lantern for the Hall, to which we had all contributed. I was very pleased to receive a book which the club presented to me at the party.

I must add that each member had a small note book presented to them. Janet, I must add, was our club second. During this year we chose Wendy as our Club Librarian as at the club's request I started a library.

[The girls wrote some items themselves, here are two examples MP]

The Cosy Cottage by Ann Parkinson

The old and cosy cottage,
That stands upon the hill,
The people there are well of age,
And everything is still.

The cottage has two rooms,
Which makes it very cosy,
And every day they use a broom,
To keep it fresh and rosy.

Outside it is so quite,
The garden smells so sweet,
The old man's name is Tony,
The woman's Margarete.

Sonnet - A Spring Morning by Pat Stacey (Captain)

How sweet the air, how bright the morning Sun,
In spring so fair the birds do sing so sweet,
All things are gay, and lambs do gaily bleat,
How still the pool, where stoats have lots of fun
And dykes where water voles so softly run.
In woods the deer, like shadows swift and fleet,
Are running to and fro on silent feet;
White snails do creep as weighted with a ton.
The crocus and the snowdrop sweetly smile,
The daffodil is dancing in the breeze;
The children hasten as they cross the style
Beneath the green of overhanging trees;
The bell is ringing so they dare not stay
The school is drab, from beauty shut away.

Sheredean Chapter 5

1950
Written by Pat Stacey, essays by Rosemary Lockley and Wendy Stacey

THE YEAR 1950 STARTED WITH an election, Ann was chosen as leader and Joy as second. They were on the committee together with Captain, José and Wendy who was the Librarian.

Good Friday Hike - 1950

On April 7th, 1950, which was a Good Friday the club went a hike to Lambley Dumbles. Captain, Ann, Margaret, José, Wendy, Janet, Gillian and myself went and here is a photo taken at the start when we were all clean and tidy! Rosemary will write about it.

It was a nice fine day and quite warm for the time of year, and as soon as we reached the Dumbles we started to collect wood for a fire, as most of us were going to cook our dinner. I had got my feet wet on the way there, so I tried to dry myself but not very successfully. After dinner (I had had sandwiches) we played rounders and had some races. We then walked into Lambley village and Captain treated us to an ice cream. Some of us had more than one, and others bought more lemonade.

We went back to the Dumbles and explored. By then it was beginning to get late, so we packed up our things and started off home. On the way, we saw some horses, and some members of the club were very frightened of them, but Margaret and I talked to the horses while the others escaped through a hole in a wired gate. We caught them up and managed the rest of the journey without incident. We had had a very nice time but were glad to get home.

Rosemary Lockley

At Whitsuntide we did some practice camping down the garden. The first night Jean and I slept in my tent on the sun bathing lawn, and José and Gillian slept in the shed on beds. The following morning (Sunday) we cooked our breakfast at the house and took it down the garden to eat. But at dinner time we cooked our dinner outside, with some of the others as well. Here is a photo of us (left to right) Wendy, Gillian, Margaret, José, Captain and Jean. We, as you can see are very busy round the fire with rather a lot of smoke.

An example of the written text in the log book

We cooked potatoes in their jackets but cooked them so well that there was hardly any potato left. We also had some tinned beans with some bacon. For afters we had a smashing steam pudding made by José, it really was delicious with syrup on it.

In the afternoon Daddy said he would take us for a ride in the car, but as there were too many of us to ride we took it in turns. It was great fun and we went quite a distance walking and riding. That night Jean, Gillian, José and I slept out again.

At 10am the following morning we met to go on a hike, we being Rosemary, Wendy, Gillian, José, Ann, Margaret, Jean and myself and my friend Shiela Headley. We went somewhere between Oxton and Calverton. When we saw a wood close at hand we decided that was the place to stop and cook our dinner. We asked some scouts that were camping there whether it would be all right and they replied 'yes' but before we had all finished cooking a scout told us that we must put the fire out and light it in a sand pit where it was safer. This we did but those who had not cooked their dinner had a job to get the fire going. The rest of us went down to Calverton Village to see the Sunday School parade. We arranged to meet the other members of the club in the Village but they turned up an hour late and so lost points for the club. Margaret was very annoyed about it (although it was her fault) so she left the club there and then. But the rest of us soon forgot about this. That night Rosemary and I slept in the tent, and Jean and Wendy slept in the shed. Here is a photo of Shiela Headley and myself (Pat) eating breakfast in the garden.

Pat, dark hair

On Thursday April 13th we all went to the Bonington Cinema to see "What a carry on" with Jimmy Jewel and Ben Warris. Club paid half the money for this outing.

We spent some of our money on a dozen boxes to sit on, and keep our folders in, down the garden. The next important event was our concert on Tuesday 29th of August. Wendy will tell you all about it.

The Club Concert - 1950

The Club Concert in 1950 was held on Tuesday 29th August at 7pm. The admission was 4d. The concert, of course, was held in the garden.

The play, which was called 'The Good Old Days' started the concert off very well indeed, and Gillian was a very good court usher, and, after a lot of practice got her 'Silence in Courts' in the right places. Joy was the Judge, and Shirley Marshall, who came up to help us with the play very good as Slick Lines. Janet, José, Ann, Jean

Sumpton and myself were also in the play.

During the concert some of us did a mime called 'The Tramp' or 'A Bench in Hyde Park'. This went off very well indeed.

Later on in the concert there were 4 dances and 8 poems. Jean Sumpton sang 'Shenandoah' and before the puppet show there was a short interval. Mr Seed had made a full size puppet theatre which was a great asset to the show. At the end of the concert we had a campfire which we all joined in. José and myself dressed up and sang 'I am a sailor young and gay' [In 1950 the word gay meant happy and full of fun MP].

After the show there was a sale of work and we made £4 to £5 on it.

We had all enjoyed the evening very much indeed and we hope that everybody who came enjoyed it also.

Wendy Stacey

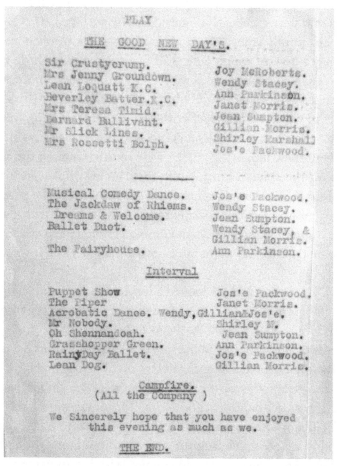

This is a picture of the typed programme for the play, I like the names of the characters
Michael Parkinson

After the concert a new member joined named Jean Roberts. Immediately after came Arnold Youth Week, and we were soon busy selling programmes for this, as it was a competition between the different youth organisations to see who could sell the most programmes. Boys Brigade came first, Red Cross second, and we were third, we sold 156 in all.

Wendy will now give a full account of the week.

ARNOLD YOUTH GALA WEEK 1950

Arnold Youth Gala Week was held from the 9th of Sep to the 17th. Margaret Worton was the Princess of Youth and she made a short speech at the Opening Display. Her attendants were 2 Red Cross girls and the Co-op provided their frocks.

On Saturday 9th, in the morning, Ann, José and myself went down to the Arnold Library to arrange things, which the club had made, for the Handwork Display by local youth. This display lasted all the week. There was a table mat and tray cloth which Captain said were excellently embroidered by me (aged 10). Captain herself sent a pair of beautifully embroidered chair backs and a woollen cushion cover. Also she sent a tea cosy to which Janet had made some sweet little egg cosies to match. Gillian sent a cushion cover as well. Our Club Leader Ann, sent a wonderfully embroidered tray cloth set. The Club was also very pleased to display a blanket made of squares to which we had all contributed. Other little items were also sent.

On Saturday afternoon there was a grand opening display in which there was a parade. A few of the Club, being guides, were in this. Later, in the afternoon we were very proud to see one of our Club in the dancing display, in the Park. This of course was José. Also there were numerous other things in the park that day in which the Club was interested especially the dancing in the evening on the lawn. Daddy was the Master of Ceremonies and he soon got it going with a swing.

I did not go on the Monday night but Captain went and said it was quite a good show.

On Tuesday, Janet, Ann and Joy looked after the Library exhibition while a few of the other members of the Club went to a dance at the Empress ballroom. Daddy was also the MC for this.

On Wednesday Daddy compered the sports at Robert Mellors School   .
Ann, Gillian and myself looked after the library on Thursday night.

Friday was the great event of the week for most of the club, as we performed a mime in the Daybrook Baptist Schoolroom. This mime was called 'The Tramp' and Joy, Ann, Gillian, José and myself were in it. Captain arranged it. Joy was a young Lady and it caused much laughter and whistling among the audience when she came on stage. Ann, who was an old woman, with lots of parcels caused much merriment also. I came in dressed as a little girl and after me, Gillian, dressed as a very good looking boy. We two played around a bit on the seat until finally José, as a tramp walked in and sat by the side of me. She started scratching her fleas and passed them on to me. Gradually she moved us all off the bench and lay down and went to sleep. This mime went off very well.

The following night there was a searchlight display. The Girl Guides sang a few songs. There were also other things that night.

To conclude the week there was a Grand Parade in which some of the Club joined.

Wendy Stacey

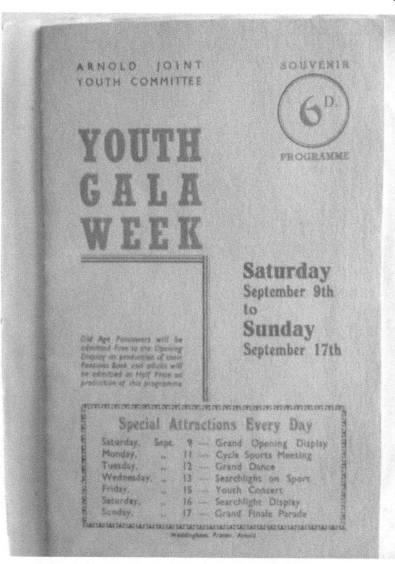

Programme for Youth Week

Message of Thanks

The Arnold Joint Youth Committee wish to express their thanks and appreciation to The Arnold Urban District Council for the numerous facilities granted and to the many ladies and gentlemen who have contributed in so many ways to this joint effort.

Signed H. CAVE.
Chairman.

In Arnold Library
September 9th to 16th

A Special Display of Handicraft and Needlework by local youth.

A Reading Display of Youth Literature will be specially arranged by C. Hargreaves, Esq. Librarian.

Page One

Squashes & Cordials

BY

Apollo

Saturday, September 9th

GRAND OPENING DISPLAY

2.30 p.m. Procession of all uniformed organisations with bands, with the Princess of Youth and Decorated Cycles, to assemble in Church Drive and parade via Mansfield Road, Daybrook Square, Nottingham Road, Front Street, Cross Street, High Street, Arnot Hill Road to rear entrance of Arnot Hill Park.

3.15 p.m. Welcoming of Princess of Youth (Miss Margaret Worton) and official opening of Garden Party by Lt./Col. S. Farr, M.C., supported by Councillor J. R. Toplis, J.P., Chairman, Arnold Urban District Council, and Councillors.

Children's Dancing Display by The Adrienne School of Dancing.
Principal: Miss Brenda Towle, F.A.A.T.D., M.R.A.D.

Physical Training Display by the Boys of Lowdham Grange.
By kind permission of the Governor H. Kenyon, Esq.

Hand Bell Ringing by Beeston Boys' Brigade

Country Dancing Display by Local School Children.

Punch and Judy Show.

7.0 p.m. Dancing on the Lawn

Numerous Sideshows and Attractions organised and operated by members of Youth Organisations.

Admission to Park   —   Adults 6d.   Children 3d.

Monday, September 11th

at 7 p.m.

CYCLE SPORTS
MEETING

on the

Gedling Rd. Recreation Ground

CYCLE POLO MATCH

Meeting arranged by the Arnold Wheelers' Cycling Club.

Tuesday, September 12th

7 to 11 p.m.

GRAND DANCE

in the

EMPRESS BALLROOM

The Arcadians Dance Band

(Members of the D.M.A.)

M.C.: A. L. Stacey, Esq.

SPOT PRIZES, Etc.

Admission - - Two Shillings

HIGH - CLASS GROCER

J. BUTTERWORTH

PROVISION MERCHANT

SUDDABY'S
FOR
CAKES

Wednesday, Sept

At 7 30 p

Searchlight on Sport at

Compere A. C

BALANCING and PYRAMIDS

WEIGHT - LIFTING

by

GEDLING YOUTH CLUB

Admission . .

ANTHONY Tel.: 67452

OF

ARNOLD

HARDWARE :: HOUSEHOLD & ELECTRICAL GOODS
PAINTS & DISTEMPERS :: "CROWN" WALLPAPERS

Page Six

September 13th

7 30 p.m.

at *Robert Mellors School*

A. L. Stacey, Esq.

VAULTING and GYMNASTICS
by
LOWDHAM GRANGE BOYS

Cycling on Rollers and other attractions

Adults 1/-   Children 6d.

Page Eight

Friday, September 15th

YOUTH
CONCERT
at 7.30 p.m.

in the

Daybrook Baptist Schoolroom

by a

★ GALAXY OF LOCAL TALENT ★

Compere: ~~A. L. Stacey~~, Esq.
W. Roper.

Admission - Adults 1/- Children 6d.

Page Nine

Saturday, September 16th

at 7.30 p.m.

Searchlight
Display

on the

Gedling Road
Recreation Ground

Display of P.T. by Boys' Brigade.

Display of Tent Pitching and Fire Lighting by Boy Scouts.

Sing - Song by Girl Guides.

Teams from all Boys' Organisations in Six-a-Side Football Match.

Display of Tumbling by Girls of Gedling Youth Club.

Display of Sectional Attack by Army Cadet Corps, etc., and other spectacular attractions.

Page Eleven

51

Sunday, September 17th
At 3.15 p.m.

GRAND
FINALE
PARADE

All uniformed organisations will parade via Mansfield Road, Daybrook Square, Nottingham Road, Front Street, Cross Street, High Street to the Bonington Theatre, other Youth Groups to assemble at the Theatre. Service to be run entirely by Youth.

All Religious Denominations are invited to take part.

Final Items In a Memorable Week

More than 150 people congregated in the Daybrook Baptist Schoolroom last Friday evening for the youth concert organised by the Arnold Joint Youth Committee as part of Arnold's Youth Gala Week.

The comprehensive programme started with a prayer followed by community singing with Mrs. T. Lockley at the piano, then Betty Wilcox and Elizabeth Atherley, both members of the Ebenezer Youth Club, gave amusing performances as Pa and Ma in the comedy sketch, "On the Sands."

A monologue by A. D. Rowland of the 26th Nottingham (Front-street Baptist) Company, The Boys' Brigade, which ensued, was well received and everyone had a lot of fun in a "Have a Go" session with Capt. W. Roper, of the Boys' Brigade, as question master. Volunteer "quiz kids" from the audience were a little shy at first, but they relaxed more and more, encouraged by the humour of Capt. Roper who made a creditable debut as an amateur comedian.

Members of the Sherdean Club in a mime entitled "The Tramp" were silently expressive, and Miss P. Stacey, who arranged the sequence, is deserving of credit.

N.C.O.'s of the Boys' Brigade with Lieut. P. Stanfield, evoked much amusement with their sketch "Officer's Nightmare," in which the awkwardness and dumbness of raw recruits was exaggerated to comic proportions. After an interval for refreshments, versatile Capt. Roper opened the second half of the entertainment with a song.

Newspaper report of Youth Week

At the end of September Jean Sumpton left the Club. Some weeks later Joy rang me to tell me about Woodthorpe Talent Night, to ask if I would like any of the club to enter. I told her I would ask them and see.

At that time we were busy making the guy for bonfire night and what a smasher he was when he was finished. A few of the Club came up on Nov 5th so we bought 5 shilling worth of fireworks between us. We had a really lovely fire and it was a long to be remembered evening.

Only four days later was the talent night and we had decided to do 'The Tramp' again and Janet was going to recite, but unfortunately Janet backed out at the last minute. The Club very much enjoyed doing it and they didn't mind in the least not winning the prize. I must say they all acted very well, as I was told by so, by several people afterwards.

Mrs Briggs asked if it would be possible for José, (helped by Wendy) to borrow the Puppet Stage, and put on a puppet show for the Children's Christmas party at the Conservative hall. This they did and the children were very thrilled.

By this time we had started learning carols, making Christmas stockings for Dr Barnardo's Homes and making arrangements for our Christmas Party. This receipt for 7/2½ is what we collected in farthings (1/2½) and some from our friends.

The Carol singing party went out twice, the first time to Ann's and Joy's and round about their districts, where we were very welcome, and invited in to share some mince pies and drinks, etc. The second night (Xmas Eve) we kept to Sandfield Road and round about. We raised even more money than before and sent £2 to Dr Barnardo's. Here is the letter from Dr Barnardo's.

DR. BARNARDO'S HOMES

NATIONAL INCORPORATED ASSOCIATION

Patrons { THEIR MAJESTIES THE KING AND QUEEN
{ HER MAJESTY QUEEN MARY

President: HER ROYAL HIGHNESS THE PRINCESS MARGARET

BARNARDO-DAY FUND

Telegrams: JONES, WAIFDOM, EDO, LONDON
Telephone: STEPNEY GREEN 3405

Chairman: BRYAN E. PIGGS, Esq.
Secretary: ANEURIN JONES, B.A.

Head Office: 18-26, STEPNEY CAUSEWAY
LONDON, E.1.

23rd January, 1951

Miss P. Stacey,
66, Sandfield Road,
Arnold.   Notts.

Dear Miss Stacey,

In forwarding to you our Honorary Treasurer's receipt for your valued contribution I should like you to know how deeply we appreciate your kindness.

As in every home throughout our land, Christmas always brings its own special responsibilities to Barnardo's also, but we rejoice in the growing number of friends whose generosity enabled us to provide our little ones with those happy times we associate so freely with the festive season.

I should like to express the hope that your Carol Party derived as much enjoyment as it gives me pleasure to acknowledge your contribution.

Please accept our renewed thanks and the good wishes of our large family of 7,000 boys and girls for the New Year.

Yours sincerely,

Aneurin Jones

Now we come to the results of the year

Attendance - Wendy with full marks (48)

Points - Wendy with 340

We bought a small Electro Plated Nickel Silver cup to be given each week for the best and quietest girl. Rosemary won this nine times so she had a prize.

Wendy gained the highest number, (46) for concert work and sale of work combined. Captain and Rosemary made the most squares for the blanket during the year (34 each). During the year we had two Silver Paper competitions. The first was won by Janet and the second by Wendy.

We would like to thank Rosemary very much, for putting the most money into the Club box, during the year. The prizes were given as usual at the Xmas party and every body received some small thing. Report by Rosemary on the party.

Christmas Party 1950

On the Tuesday before Christmas we held our Christmas Party. All the Club members came and we had a very nice time and a grand tea. Shirley Marshall, who helped in the summer concert, was a guest, and we also invited Mr and Mrs Seed to the party. Mr Seed had very kindly made a puppet theatre for us, and as a token of appreciation we gave him 20 Players cigarettes. We gave Mr Stacey 1oz of St Julian tobacco, and Mrs Stacey a calendar. After tea, we all played games. Mr Stacey made us all very frightened by pretending to give us an electric shock with some wire (not real of course, but we did not know that). We all had a very good time, and when the party ended, we were all very sorry. Everyone looked forward to the next one, and hoped it would be as great a success.

Rosemary Lockley

Sheredean Chapter 6

1951

Written by Pat Stacey, essays, Ann Parkinson, Gillian Morris, Wendy Stacey and Betty Shaw

THE COMMITTEE CHOSEN WAS CAPTAIN, Ann and Joy selected and Rosemary made secretary, we had closed the library down as Wendy said she was not doing much trade.

But at Ann's request I started a club bank, any of the club could join even if it was for a penny a week.

At the beginning of February we had a new member join (Valentine Thompson). Two weeks later Rosemary Neal who was called Rosemary number 2 joined. And at the beginning of April Rosemary 2 bought her friend Betty Shaw to join. They were only nine years old. Ann will tell about our hike at Easter.

Good Friday Hike (1951)

On Good Friday the club went on a hike to Lambley Dumbles they were Wendy, Val, Gill, Rosemary, Joy, Captain and myself. The weather was not very nice. But we set out to make the most of it. It did not rain much while we were going and when we arrived we played down the Dumbles for about half an hour getting very muddy and Wendy fell down and lost her hat in the stream. When we had just got the fire alight, down it came, rain, sleet and snow. We finished our dinner hurriedly and set out for home. We had to face the rain most of the way and before we were even half way home we were soaked and in the end we walked through puddles instead of trying to avoid them. When we got back Mrs Stacey provide some of us with skirts, jumpers and shoes while our own dried.

Ann Parkinson

At the end of April, two more girls joined, Meresia Ellis and Julie Palmer. We decided that at Whitsun we would like to go camping. So one day Daddy took me to see Mrs Fox who lived at a farm on the Ollerton Road. But unfortunately she could not have us there as the owner of the farm would not allow camping. But she suggested that we should try Mr Slack at Catcliffe Hill Farm (Arnold) which was not very far away from there. This we did and he said we could have a field there. So we got cracking and advertised for a tent. We succeeded in getting quite a nice bell tent with every thing belonging to it including a large ground sheet all for £4. Then we bought 10 yards of hessian, to make some screening, dixie frying pan, 3 cape ground sheets, mallet, rope, jugs basins, dairy cloth for covering things and other small items, other things we had given to us or borrowed for the weekend.

The Thursday before Whitsun, Ann, Gillian and I went out there on our bikes with two spades to dig the fireplace, grease pits and latrines. Now we will write a full report of the Camp and Camp site.

(There was no report in the book but there were some photographs MP).

On the lorry taking us to camp

we returned we sent some

Enjoying ourselves at camp

When we returned we sent some tobacco to Mr Slack, thanking him for letting him us have the site. This is the poem we sent with it:-

> Here's to the farmer who's always Slack,
> Takes from the land but puts it back,
> Genial and friendly and never a damper,
> Encouraging and helpful to every camper,
> Here's to the health of our very good friend;
> We hope this 'baccys' a suitable blend.

(by A.L.Stacey)

We also gave Mr Rowley 20 'cigs' for taking us and bringing us back in his lorry. We had a silver paper competition on June 5th which Wendy won.

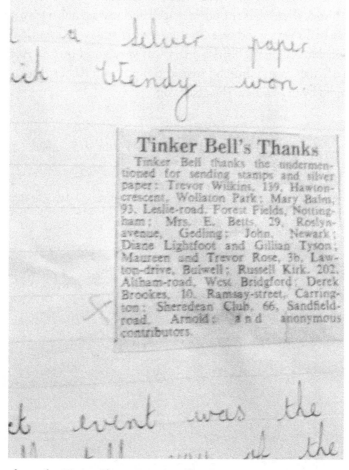

Tinker Bell's Thanks

Tinker Bell thanks the undermentioned for sending stamps and silver paper: Trevor Wilkins, 159, Hawton-crescent, Wollaton Park; Mary Bain, 93, Leslie-road, Forest Fields, Nottingham; Mrs. E. Betts, 29, Roslyn-avenue, Gedling; John, Newark; Diane Lightfoot and Gillian Tyson; Maureen and Trevor Rose, 3b, Lawton-drive, Bulwell; Russell Kirk, 202, Aldham-road, West Bridgford; Derek Brookes, 10, Ramsay-street, Carrington; Sheredean Club, 66, Sandfield-road, Arnold; and anonymous contributors.

A cutting from the Nottingham Evening Post.

The next event was the Youth Gala Week. Ann will tell you of the part we played on the day of the opening display.

The opening of the Youth Gala Week (1951)

At the opening of the Youth Gala Week, some of our members were present. They were Val, Wendy, Janet and myself. We went to help Mr Henstock to sell tickets for the activities of the following week. I wrote and stamped some tickets for the Lowdham Grange Boys, (Lowdham Grange was a borstal institution MP) and for the Women's League of Heath and Beauty. Although we did not sell many tickets we tried very hard and were rewarded with a 'Free Tea'. After that we had finished our set job so Janet and Val went home, and Wendy and I stayed for the dancing. We were joined by Cap, José and Gill. Captain and I sold the tickets for dancing and afterwards joined in.

On the Sunday although it rained a little we had quite a pleasant evening service in the park. Monday evening went off very well and it was such a pity it wasn't well supported as we had a very good cast. Among the artistes were Bonnie Forest, a well known singer in Nottingham. Shirley Hart was very good on the Accordion and piano. A team of Girls from Church Drive and Boys from Robert Mellors took part in a quiz arranged by my Father. The girls won.

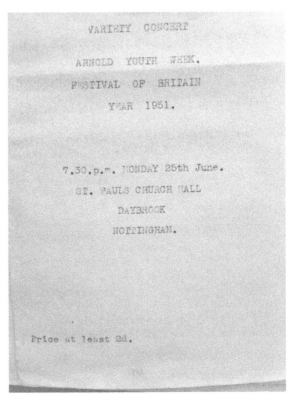

```
            VARIETY  CONCERT

        ARNOLD   YOUTH   WEEK.

        FESTIVAL  OF  BRITAIN

              YEAR  1951.



      7.30.p.m. MONDAY 25th June.

        ST. PAULS CHURCH HALL

              DAYBROOK

              NOTTINGHAM.




    Price at least 2d.
```

PROGRAMME

COMPARE - GEORGE NICKLING ESQ.,(CENTRAL COUNCIL FOR PHYSICAL RECREATION)

1. Vaulting & Gymnastic Display
   by Lowdham Orange Boys.

2. Weight Lifting
   by Gedling Youth Club.

3. Wrestling
   by Central Council for
   Physical Recreation.

4. Balancing & Pyramids.
   by Gedling Youth Club.

5. High Bars.
   By Nottingham Gymnastic Club.

6. Jui-Jitsu & Judo
   By Nottingham School of Judo
   and Jui-Jitsu.

7. Netball Match.
   Hucknall Nationals
   v
   Carlton County Secondary Girl
   School.

Have you secured your tickets yet for

(a) The Swimming Gala tomorrow starting at 7.30.p.m?

(b) The Olde Tyme Dance on Friday in this School Hall?

Don't delay - tickets are on sale here and now.

This is what the typed programme looked like

Being Club night, and very busy practising for the concert, none of us went to hear the Hames Hague Accordion Band. But people who went said it was quite a success. Wednesday nights programme was also quite an enjoyable one. I thought the Gymnastic display was excellent.

As Gillian entered for the Swimming races, she will tell you what it was like.

Swimming Gala

Thursday came which was the night I was to swim in the gala. Crowds waited outside the dressing rooms to change to swim. All was well till I saw the girls I was competing against then my heart went in my mouth. I got changed then went out to see the others race but the first sight of the people made me shiver. Race after race went by until at last the time came. I threw my towel from my shoulder and went to the starting point. Everyone got ready for the signal "go' and we were off. By this time the water was very rough and was a job to keep my head above it.

Gillian Morris

(Gillian finished her story here, I think because she got to the bottom of the page MP)

G. Morris   No. 56
A. Parkinson. No. 57.

ARNOLD JOINT YOUTH COMMITTEE

Second Annual Swimming Gala

Under A.S.A. Laws.

Thursday 28th June, 1951.

Commencing at 7-30 pm

at the

PUBLIC BATHS, ARNOLD.

Presentation of prizes by

Councillor H. Cave.

OFFICIALS:

Starter; H.S. Stretton. Esq.,
Judges. J.J.Baker,Esq.,R.H. Sulley Esq.
          J. Perkins. esq.,
Recorders: E.Headley.Esq.,H. Henstock
                                    Esq.,
Girls Steward: Miss. D. Clemence.
Boys Stewards: J. Hart.esq., S. Pacey.
                                    Esq.,
Door Steward: J.Jew esq., J.Roper.Esq.

Programme Twopence.

	Club.	No.		Club.
R. Wilkinson.	504. British Red Cross.	40. G. Beattie.	1st. Woodthorpe Boy Scouts
A. Berridge.	" " " "	41. C. Turpin.	" " " "
K. Kirk.	" " " "	42. Lockwood.	" " " "
W. Godfrey.	" " " "	43. Marshallneigh"	" " " "
D. Hopton.	" " " "	44. R. Hardy.	1st. Arnold Girl Guides.
A. Bursey.	" " " "	45. Margaret Parkin	" " " "
M. Hatchar,	" " " "	46. Monica Parkin	" " " "
G. Halford.	26 Coy Boys Brigade.	47. J. Gasgoine.	" " " "
D. Raymond.	" " " "	48. J. Furzius.	" " " "
R. Baker.	" " " "	49. P. Asher.	" " " "
T. Hardy.	" " " "	50. H. Unwin.	1st. Daybrook Boy Scouts.
J.R.Toplington.	" " "	51. C. Conduit.	" " " "
Jeffrey Hopewell.	" " " "	52. K. Green.	Arnbrook Boys Club.
G. Corah.	" " "	53. J. Wild.	" " " "
John Hopewell.	" " " "	54. J. Williamson.	" " " "
J. Briggs.	" " "	55. R. Tolley.	" " " "
D. Goodwin.	" " "	56. G. Morris.	Sheredean Girls Club.
A. Sims.	Army Cadet Corps.	57. A. Parkinson.	" " " "
P. Perry.	" " "		
Grant.	Air Training Corps.		
Bakewell.	" " "		
Nathan.	" " "		
Howkins.	" " "		
J. Bridges.	" " "		
D. Hodgson.	" " "		
A. Hatton.	" " "		
T. Carmody	" " "		
E. Shaw.	2nd Arnold Boy Scouts.		
N.W.Seagrave.	" " "		
A.E.Hardy.	" " "		
J. Gosling.	" " "		
R. Berrington.	" " "		
C. Pickering.	" " "		
F. Pindar.	" " "		
R. Bruce.	" " "		
Hart.	" " "		
R. Martin.	" " "		
R. Wilson.	" " "		
C. Palethorpe.	" " "		

May we take this opportunity of
reminding you of the following event:

Olde Tyme Dance. Robert Mellors School
Friday 20th June.

Youth Service.
Front Street Baptist Church.
Sunday 1st July.

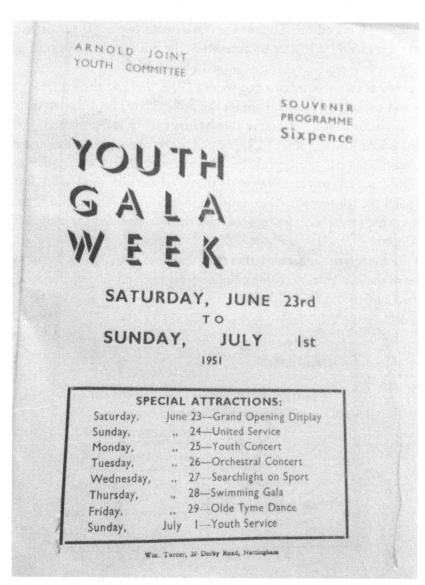

Front of Gala Week Programme

The Club Concert 1951

The club concert 1951 was held in July. It began at seven o'clock on a very pleasant evening, although it was a bit cold and many people came along quickly and took their places in the audience.

The concert commenced with the Opening Chorus and was followed by the play which was called 'Before the play'. This, I think went off very well and José was good as George. She forgot her beard and I had to whisk on and give it to her. After a lot of practising Gill and Ann tumbled over properly on the day. The play is taking place backstage. It is a rehearsal before the play actually begins. The poor producer, Miss Brown, is in a terrible state because Mary, the princess does not turn up, and everything goes wrong.

This play was followed by two poems, one "The Owl and the Pussycat' recited by Betty and the other by Janet. Later in the programme José did a tap dance and another delightful dance, but before this however six of us performed 'A visit to the Ballet' which José of course had arranged for us. Ann and Gillian and myself recited and the puppet show, performed by José and Gillian, went off very well. 'The Doctors Surgery' was excellent, and I think Val was very good as the deaf man.

We ended the concert with a campfire in which we all joined, and some of us sang solos, which were well appreciated, and then we finished the show with the Ending Chorus.

After the concert the audience either tried their luck at the sideshows or went in the house to the sale of work. I think this concert went off very well indeed and I feel sure the audience agreed with me.

Wendy Stacey

The concert programme 1951

Again we made about £5. Everyone seemed to have enjoyed it and thought we had done very well especially for such a small Club.

After the concert was over Ann and I went camping together into Derbyshire. We borrowed the Clubs equipment for the week and managed to give the Club 7/-3d for the loan of it. Shiela Headley and Dorothy Sale also went with us.

Here are some photos.

Back left to right Pat and Shiela, front Ann and Dorothy

Ann Parkinson

The Camp Field

The same week that we returned from camp (Bank Holiday Week) we took the Club for mystery outing which the Club paid for.

Well here we are at Clifton by the river, we spent the afternoon paddling in a stream which runs by the river. Here we were busy sucking iced suckers, and ice creams, and sunning ourselves, yes, it really was a lovely summers day and we had a jolly good time, but its not like the Club to keep dry, so we just had to have a good old storm to finish us off; we sheltered for some time but you should have seen us walking through town with towels round our heads. (But our spirits were not dampened)!

At Clifton before the storm

At the end of August, Janet left the club, I thought I would like a little more help with the Club, so I asked Ann to be Vice Captain which she did very willingly. The Club made Joy their leader and Gillian their second.

The Club again made a smashing Guy for the Bonfire, and helped a lot by carting stuff across to the stack on the Lamus. (the Lamus was an area of waste ground in Arnold MP). We bought 5/s worth of fireworks including some sparklers for the younger ones which we older ones!! enjoyed just as much. We had a good fire although it teamed down with rain all the evening and we went home wet through. I'm pleased to say we were none the worse for our wetting as the Club it seems are used to getting wet!

I had a lot of old cards and pictures so we decided to make some scrap books for the Children's Hospital, which we did and at Christmas we sent off about 8 lovely books. This is the letter we received from the Hospital.

HOSPITAL MANAGEMENT COMMITTEE
No. 2.

MATRON'S OFFICE.   NOTTINGHAM CHILDREN'S HOSPITAL,
                                               NOTTINGHAM.
    —
                                          TELEPHONE NO. 65065-6.
    MATRON :
MISS M. A. BODEN.

    IEH/LB   17th December, 1951.

Miss P. Stacey,
Sheredean Club,
Sandfield Road,
ARNOLD, Notts:

Dear Miss Stacey,

    Will you please convey to the members of your Club the sincere thanks of all our children for the attractive Scrap Books which they have so kindly sent to the hospital ?

    These books will be greatly appreciated by the patients here this Christmas and I am very grateful for your kind thought for us at this season.

            Yours sincerely,

            J. E. Hawkins

    Assistant Matron.

Another silver paper collection was sent up to Tinker Bell

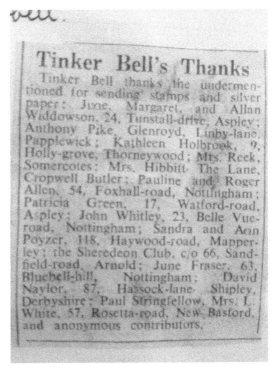

Another cutting from the Nottingham Evening Post

As usual we made Xmas stockings for Dr Barnardo's, collected 1/6 worth of farthings plus10/-6 on my Xmas tree collection (The receipt was for 12/6d MP)

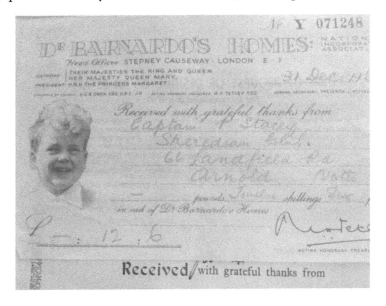

T .12145

Received Jan 4th 1952 with grateful thanks from

The Club. "Skeredean",
Per S. Stacey (Captain)

G/c. of —
22. Gifts —
Books, Decorations.
Games, Xmas Stockings
Toys. Etc.

73

The Tuesday before Christmas was our Ranger Company's Concert at the Scout Hall in Nottingham. We decided if we wanted to have Club together we would have to take the Club to the concert, as both Vice Cap and I were in it. This we did instead of giving a small present each for Xmas, and we paid for the outing, which I think we all enjoyed.

The following Thursday was the Christmas party and Betty is going to write a little about it.

The Christmas Party 1951

First of all we played a few games and we had tea. We had jellies cakes and sandwiches. After tea we played black magic and white magic. Rosemary Neal trod on Mr Staceys poor little toe. Then we had a game of balloons. I won a prize and so did Rosemary.

We gave captains mother and father a present for letting us have club in the front room. We gave captain a present as well. In the evening we had prize-giving and cap will put down who won.

Betty Shaw (age 9 MP)

Attendance
Rosemary Lockley - 44 out of 45
Wendy Stacey - 44 out of 45
Points
Wendy Stacey with 247 points
Cup Winner
Wendy Stacey who won the cup 15 times
Squares
Janet Morris 24 made during the year
(These were knitted squares which were joined together to form blankets MP)
A big thank you went to Rosemary Lockley for putting in 10/10 during the year, over half as much more than anyone else in the Club.

On the following Saturday we went Carol Singing and again did very well as you will see from the receipt over leaf.

One house we went in, and sang to them inside; they had a party on, and they were very pleased to see us especially when we sang 'We Three Kings' with Vice Cap, Wendy and little Betty singing solos which sounded very nice. We went into several houses and were offered Mince Pies, tarts and drinks which were very welcome. But the most exciting part was when we got home and counted the money, we were pleased with our nights work and felt we had really done some good for Dr Barnardo's.

Here are some pictures of Dr Barnardo's children whom we try and help.

Citizens of the future at one of our Schoolboys' Homes.

In Dr. Barnardo's great family of 7,000 children there are more than a thousand babies, tweenies and toddlers.

Sea-dogs all ! We maintain a Sea-training School where boys are taught the rudiments of seafaring life at the hands of qualified seamen.

All set for a spell of gardening?

Happiness is the key-note in Dr. Barnardo's Homes and our Nurseries ring with the chuckles of tiny tots.

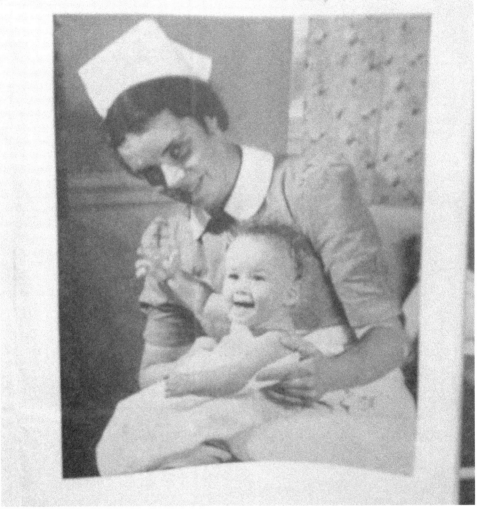

These pictures were all sent to the Sheredean Club by Dr Barnardo's

Sheredean Chapter 7

1952

Written by Pat Stacey, essays, Ann Parkinson, Pat Stacey, Rosemary Lockley and Meresia Ellis

THE COMMITTEE FOR 1952 WAS - Rosemary Lockley elected Leader and secretary and Gillian as second. The first thing to remember this year is how two children, namely Wendy and Gillian, kept the 2nd club rule by helping to save a dog, here is the newspaper cutting about it.

> **NOTTM. G.M. SAVES DOG FROM POND**
>
> Thirty-three year-old P.C. Hugh Douglas, of Nottingham City Police, who last year recived the George Medal for saving a child from fire, yesterday saved a dog from water. He waded neck deep into the water of a brickpond at Mapperley to save the dog, a cross-bred cocker. The animal fell into the water when thin ice covering the pond gave way.
>
> "Two children came to tell me that the dog was in the water and I went to the pond with some ladders," P.c. Douglas told the Post. "I could not use them, however, and waded in. The dog was about 10 to 12 yards out and I was glad the water did not get any deeper."
>
> After the rescue, P.c. Douglas returned to his home at 211. Woodborough-road, changed into dry clothes, and returned to duty.
>
> P.c. Douglas received the George Medal in October for saving a child from a burning house in Peashill-road Nottingham, after the father and two other men had been forced back by flames.

In March Gillian brought a new girl named Delia, but she only came for a few weeks.

Here is an Easter photo of Gillian.

The next happy event was our usual outing on Good Friday, Ann will tell us about it.

On Good Friday, 11th April, the club went on a hike to Lambley Dumbles. The weather looked very promising and we set off at 10-15. We were, Betty, Rosemary 2, Delia, Julie, Val, Wendy, Gill, Captain and myself.

We arrived at Lambley at 11-05. After a refreshment we went to look at the Dumbles and Val started off by sliding down a bank. We had our dinner at twelve to one o'clock and afterwards some of us went to Lambley Village.

When we all got together again we had a good game of cricket and three small boys came to watch us and as they did not know our names they gave some of us nicknames. Wendy - Cinderella, Val - Curley, and Captain - Stainless. We then had some tea and returned home.

Ann Parkinson

The girls at Lambley Dumbles

The fire

After this we knuckled down to some concert work, which we did willingly, thinking ahead of the Club camp, and outing which was to follow.

Club Concert 1952

On Tuesday, 8th July, the Club held their annual concert and sale of work. It was a warm, dry night, and we had a large audience. A copy of the programme is on the next page.

During the interval we had the draw for a raffle we had arranged. The prize was a large basket of fruit, which Mrs Packwood won, a box of chocolates, a propelling pencil, and a basket of raspberries were the other prizes. During the sale, competitions were held outside for the children. There was a throwing the hoop on the board; penny in the bucket; and a bran-tub. The whole evening was a great success and the total amount made from the concert, sale and raffle was over £6.

Rosemary Lockley

The Programme - 1952

The girls at a club night in 1952

Derbyshire Camp - 1952

This camp really was fun, and the four of us who went, (V Captain, Gillian, Meresia Ellis and myself) thoroughly enjoyed ourselves. We sent most of the equipment on before hand and we went by bus, as it was a Sunday and there were no trains running to Alsop en le Dale station which was the nearest station to Alstonefield (3 miles away). Unfortunately we could only get a bus as far as there, and it took us ages and ages to walk to the camp site as it was all up hill and very hard going, with our kit.

Then came the struggle with the tent, as by this time we were weary, it was raining a little and blowing a lot. But it was soon up and we got it ship shape pretty quickly, we borrowed some poles and made a good fire shelter, and dug the Latrines and got the store tent into order, then to bed.

We awoke to find it rather wet and very cold to the feet on Monday morning, but Tuesday proved to be a marvellous day, so we packed our lunch and started off for Dovedale, we walked right through the dale and then climbed Thorpe Cloud, and walked all the way back (about ten miles altogether).

Wednesday was Visitors day so we stayed in camp all day, it was a very good camp site, the snags being wood!!! and rain water only unless you bought fresh water off the lorry each morning.

The only visitors were Mr and Mrs Ellis and family who did not stop many minutes, but they nearly took Gillian back with them as she had been in bed ill all day, but I thought she would be better in the morning so she stayed with us.

On Thursday the weather was again lovely so we set off for the Manifold Vally leaving Gillian behind because she did not feel like walking.

Pat Stacey

The Manifold Valley

Gillian was ill in camp, so Cap, Ann and myself set off to the Manifold Valley. It was about five miles and to reach it we had to pass through Wetton, where we stopped to have a sucker.

The Manifold Valley was very low and we had to go down an enormous hill to reach it, cars often came down when they wanted to go to Wetton Mill or other places. Once there was a miniature railway right through the valley, but it is now a footpath.

We saw Thors Cave and we were going to climb it, but it was so hot that we decided not to. We crossed over the bridge 100 or so yards from Wetton Mill and watched where the River Dove went underground. Then we saw a scout camp, it was from Northampton and as it was evidently rest hour, we got by safely - much to Ann's disappointment.

Then we stopped by a ford at Wetton Mill and rested for about ¼ hour. All around us were the hills, silent and dark, so that if there were no people or cars there, only you, the silence would be almost overpowering.

After the ¼ hour was up, we paddled in the ford, and while still in the water took some snaps which turned out to be very good. Cap and I went to Wetton Mill to have a drink and were kept entertained by a dear little kitten which we kept calling names, trying to find the right one, but never succeeded.

After that we went back to find Ann sunbathing so we followed suit and got quite brown. At last Cap thought it was time to come away, so we gathered our belongings together and came. On the way back we found the scout camp alive and busy and as we were going by we saw someone practising their semaphore, then we crossed the bridge and saw two of the scouts waving to us, so of course we waved back. To make matters worse one even took out his field glasses and had a good look at us. Anyway we escaped at last. On returning we stopped at a gate and rested. I left my coat behind and only after about ten minutes did I notice it. When I went back to the spot I bumped into a party of scouts coming up the hill. I picked up my coat and got up the hill in record time while Ann and Cap stood there laughing at me. We left the scouts behind at Wetton Village where they went into the general stores.

About ½ mile from camp we made friends with a horse and spent quite a lot of time with him. But all too soon we reached camp and although we should have liked to have stayed longer we tumbled into our sleeping bags very thankfully, and we were lost in slumber among the silent hills.

Meresia Ellis

Well, that sounded, and was a very successful day. On Friday Meresia and I went to the station to see about the luggage going back and in the mean time the other two stitched up our nightclothes, at which we were not very surprised as we had expected it one night. The last night we had a midnight feast, and Derek brought my light weight tent up, and stopped the night. He proved very useful when it came to packing up on Sunday, but on Sunday morning Derek, Meresia and I went to Church, not in our Sunday best but still we went. But all too soon we were back home again, but with good photos, happy memory's and good health.

Captain

Paddling in the ford at Wetton

Last dinner in camp

Helping the farmer

Outing to Mablethorpe

On Sunday 27th July 1952, the Club went an outing to Mablethorpe. We left Victoria station at 10-20am and arrived at our destination about 1pm. We ate our lunch on the sand hills and afterwards some of the Club went in the sea. As it was rather showery and there was a cold wind, we spent the rest of the afternoon at the funfair. We went on the Whirl, the Noah's Ark and the Horses, and some of us went on the Big Wheel. We had tea at a fish and chip shop, and then some of the club decided they would like to bathe again. By the time they were dressed again it was time to return to the station.

We caught the train all right and had a very pleasant journey back to Nottingham, as a party of boys from further down the train came and joined us. We arrived at Victoria at 10-50pm (25 minutes late) and were met by Mr Stacey and Mrs Morris who very kindly took us home by car. We had all had a very enjoyable time and are looking forward to next years outing.

Rosemary Lockley

PS In January 1953, Mablethorpe suffered great damage from flooding by the sea, so we shall never again see it as it was then, and can only rely on happy memories. *RL*

The October Silver paper Competition was won by Rosemary Lockley. We have now started collecting Silver milk tops and Wendy has collected the most so far. Just before Christmas we made a children's Xmas stocking and sent this, together with some farthings, books and other articles to Dr Barnardo's Homes.

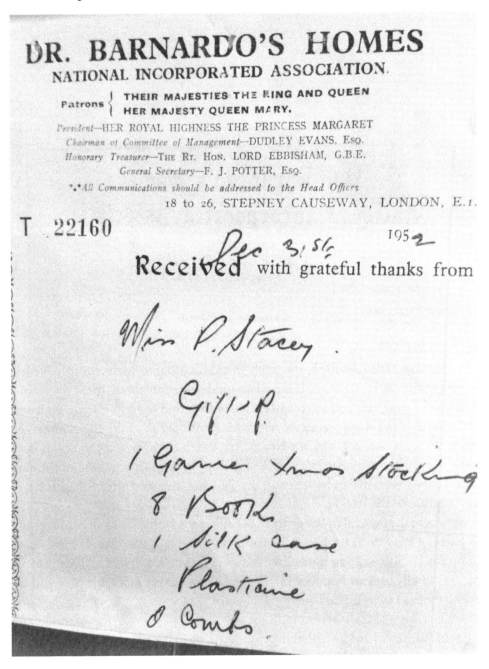

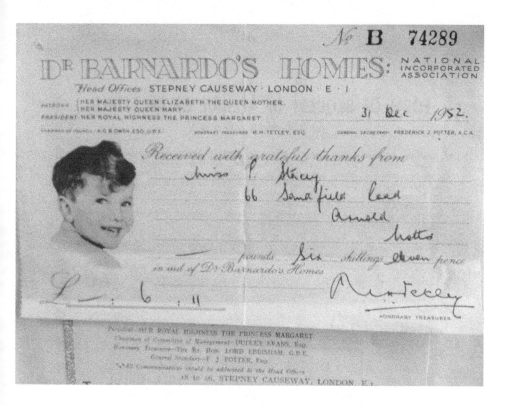

To end the year we had our usual Christmas party, to which we invited Mr & Mrs Stacey and presented them with a table runner. During the year Rosemary Lockley, (one of our oldest members) Gillian Morris, Val Thompson, Julie Palmer and Delia Beardsley all left the club but of course we invited them back for the party, and most of them came and enjoyed themselves.

The results were as follows:-

Attendance - Wendy - 41 out of 42
Points - Wendy - 227
Cup winner - Betty - 9 times
Squares - Rosemary Lockley - 6 squares

Again we say thank you to Rosemary for the money she put into the Club box. The total for the Club was £2-4-10½d. I was also given a present by the Club.

Our last good turn of the year was our Carol singing effort, which we enjoyed very much especially when we went to the Conservative Hall and sang our Carols at the children's party which the Forest Supporters Club were having. We all had what we wanted to eat and drink, and took our tin round, and came away very happy, with an orange each and our tin quite heavy.

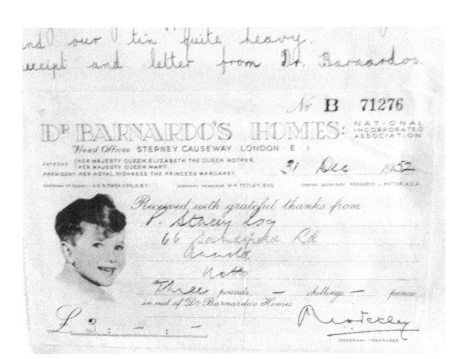

The heavy tin contained £3

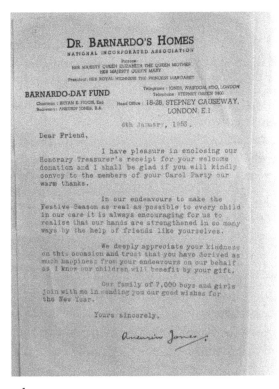

A nice thank you letter

Sheredean Chapter 8

1953

Written by Pat Stacey, essays, Meresia Ellis, Ann Parkinson and Wendy Stacey

THE 1953 COMMITTEE WERE CAPTAIN, Vice Captain as secretary, and Wendy as leader. At this time there were only six of us in the club.

No Easter outings were arranged, but that was made up for by all the Club going to camp at Whitsun time. We found a lovely site at Oxton, after hunting all over Houghton (near Southwell) where it seemed nobody had a suitable camping site. We had wonderful weather and all enjoyed themselves except Wendy who had a bad cold. Meresia tells us about it.

Oxton Camp

On Friday night we set out on a camp which proved to be very enjoyable, as you will see by the amount of things we did.

Captain and myself went by bus in peace and comfort while the others squashed themselves in the van that was to carry the luggage. The first night at camp was very uncomfortable for some of us, as we either slept in a hump or hollow, but in time we got hardened to it, and finished the rest of the stay in comfort.

The days on the whole were warm, but on the Wednesday we experienced a dreadful thunderstorm, the result of which I developed a cold, Ann's parents came over and so did Betty's, they were both caught on the way. However a steaming cup of Milo and some biscuits soon made all cheerful.

One evening when it was growing dusk, leaving the others in the tent, Cap Ann and myself went a long walk into the countryside around. We saw literally millions of rabbits playing around in the grass, and a fox and cubs run through the bracken down the hillside and into a wood below. We had a gorgeous time stalking rabbits on our stomachs and actually got within 2 yards of one which was calmly washing itself. We found a clean water spring and washed our faces, for as you will probably know it gives one a lovely complexion.

Another day we spent picnicking and exploring, we found a lake, and paddled in a stream which found its source there and took some snaps which will be shown below.

Fetching water was quite a big thing as we had to pass through a field full of young bullocks which were very frisky, or the alternative, pigs, but apart from these slight blemishes, we enjoyed every minute of it.

The daughter at the farm was getting married, while we were there, and some of us saw the wedding cake, Betty asked how many 'Storeys' there were meaning tiers, and was very pleased to find it had three.

All too soon we had to pack, and we arrived in Nottingham about 9pm and Mr Stacey and Mrs Morris fetched us in their cars. Shown below are some of the snaps, and you will see from our happy faces that we all had a jolly good time.

Meresia Ellis

The page of pictures

After this very pleasant and happy camp, we began to think about some new members, as for one thing we hadn't enough members to get up a concert. In June Ann Taylor joined us, and we started a Junior Club and Pat Ellis, Pat Roles, Mavis Roles and Penny Hill were soon enrolled with Sheredean Club badges only smaller than the Seniors. Junior time was 6 to 7pm and the Seniors 7 to 8-30pm, Tuesday nights as usual.

On June the 20th we set off on a new adventure, 'Youth Hostelling', and Wendy, as she told us about Shining Cliff, (not the best of Hostels) is writing about this weekend and the photos will follow.

Shining Cliff

Betty, Cap, VC, Meresia and myself went to the Shining Cliff Youth Hostel on June 20th, by coach to Ambergate, and then we found our way through the woods and the wire works up to the hostel, which consists of about five wooden shacks looking out over the woods with some huge stone cliffs touching behind them. We went into somebody's back garden, in the woods before we got there, and although it said two miles on the signpost, it seemed a lot more to us as it was growing late.

However we arrived, cooked our supper (baked beans and cocoa, I think) and went to bed. Meresia, Betty and I went into one hut and Cap, and VC in a larger one, and then at least, fell asleep almost directly. The following morning we cooked breakfast and did several odd jobs about the hostel, and then we got our packed lunches and set off for a days walking. I said there was a lake in the woods, but nobody believed me and we never found it. We went up higher, out of the woods and went through a private deer park, but we saw no deer. Then we came out onto a road and met some other people whom we had seen in the hostel. We joined up with them, who thought they understood maps! However we went through fields and into some woods, through a marshy place and onto a road again. We continued down this road by ourselves and found a small ford where we paddled and ate our dinner which consisted of dry bread and lettuce and marmalade. Cap and VC had great difficulty in finding the right road back. We started off along one twice, but decided to turn back and it was just as well that we did, since it was the wrong one. We found another road which finally led us back opposite the park gates and hence we went back into the woods, where we had tea, and on to Ambergate where, although the busses were full, we managed to get on safely and arrived home about 8-30pm.

I enjoyed myself very much but nobody else seemed to enjoy the Hostel where we stayed, although they enjoyed the walking, I think.

Wendy Stacey

Taken in the Deer Park

Soon after this the Seniors went to spend a pleasant Tuesday Evening on the River Trent. I think Meresia has something to say about this trip.

River Trent Trip

Last June 1953, Club set off for a trip on the River Trent, it was a fine evening and we were all in good spirits as we set off.

We practically had the boat to ourselves, which was probably lucky for the people who weren't there, as most of the Club were soaking wet through by the time we got back, owing to Betty Shaw, Ann Parkinson, Rosemary Neale and myself who would persist in dragging our hands through the water and also skimming, sending a shower over the unfortunate person in the way.

When we got back, we were very cold and wet, so some sensible people had an ice cream to hot themselves, while others indulged themselves in a steaming cup of tea out of a very greasy looking cup.

Then we decided to have a game, and finally ended up singing on the bus that carried us homewards.

Meresia Ellis

On July 18 and 19th we had a little camp down the garden with Ann and Rosemary in the little tent, and I slept in the shed, and I think we all got quite a thrill out of it, we cooked our own Sunday dinner which was jolly good.

Camping down the garden

We did not have a meeting in August, but a few of us did go for a little picnic on August 11th as you can see from the photo over page.

Penny, Wendy, Rosemary & Ann Taylor.

Then on Sunday September 6th we set off to see Dr Barnardo's Homes at Holbrook (near Derby) and Vice Captain is going to give a write up on this.

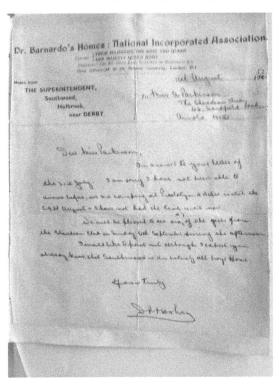

Letter from Dr Barnardo's

Visit to Dr Barnardo's Home at Holbrook

The weather looked rather doubtful as we set off to see the Doctor Barnardo's Home, but the rain did manage to keep off. We were, Cap, Wendy, Betty, Pat Ellis and myself. We had an interesting bus ride to Derby where we changed and caught an Ockbrook bus . The conductor told us where to get off.

The Dr Barnardo's Home looked just like a large old house of grey stone. When we went inside we noticed how well looked after everything seemed to be. We were greeted by an old man who asked us to wait a moment while he went to fetch a boy of about fourteen years of age, who was to show us round the place.

There were three dormitories, one in Pink, one Green and one Blue, we were also shown the room where the boys had their meals and then shown the kitchens and we saw how spotlessly clean they were. While we were on our travels we passed a small boy in the corridor who had been sent out of one of the rooms and he was looking very sorry for himself. We were told that the boys went to various schools round about so that they could mix with other children and if they passed the exams they were allowed to go to the Grammar Schools. We were by then beginning to wonder where the boys were at the present time and we found out that they were all in the Common Room enjoying themselves in some way or another.

We then went out into the garden and we discovered that the boys who wanted, had a piece of garden to look after. There were also greenhouses, inside which there were the most beautiful grapes. We were introduced to the boys' pony that someone had given to them at some time and we were told that it was the duty of one boy to look after it. When we had toured the garden we went back to the house and said our goodbyes and then set of for home and we discussed what we had seen and like most about the home on our way back.

Ann Parkinson (Vice Captain)

As I write in 2019 the buildings are now occupied by The Holbrook School for Autism.

Michael Parkinson

Janet, Pat, Pat, Penny, Mavis.

This picture was taken on Sept 8th 1953 where, as you can see Janet Athey joined the happy, or should I say noisy Juniors, and the following week Jennifer Thomas joined making 6 Juniors in all. Then down to work for the Winter Concert, as we didn't have a summer one we decided to have one nearer Christmas, and have a few new ideas, and better chance of selling also the blanket, made of squares. Well, I must say no more as Meresia has this all in hand.

Concert 1953

This concert was held in the Conservative Hall, it began at 7-15pm preceded by a sale of work which began at 6-30pm. We had an audience of about 70-80 people who helped the proceeds enormously.

The concert commenced with the opening chorus followed by a small play called 'Late'.

Next came José's dance, as she is not a club member she appeared as a guest artist. Also we invited Edgar Bentley who is a ventriloquist to put a show of his own on, which he did and I must add that he gave it for charity.

Pat and Mavis Roles came next, they said a poem, which was followed by a Puppet Sketch of 'Little Red Riding Hood', which the youngest of the audience enjoyed, judging by the 'oohs and aahs' we heard. Then came a duet by Rosemary Neal and Betty Shaw called 'The Fairy on the Christmas Tree' accompanied by a little dance performed by the same.

Most of the music accompaniment was played by Mrs Lockley. One original item on the programme was the 'Can Can', and I must say it was great fun to do. The song of the 'Tritch Tratch' and also 'Vilja' was sung by Pat Stacey, followed by Ann Parkinson who sang 'Waltz of my Heart' and said that very long poem called 'The Highwayman'.

To finish with there was the 'Christmas Mime' in which the Juniors appeared as Angels, and I must say they looked very Angelic. After a very happy time and a hectic one too for Club Members it finally finished with the ending chorus.

Oh and I must add, that in spite of all Derek's assertions the curtains of the stage finished up upside down and back to front, but nobody seemed to notice, although they looked pretty awful from the back.

Meresia Ellis

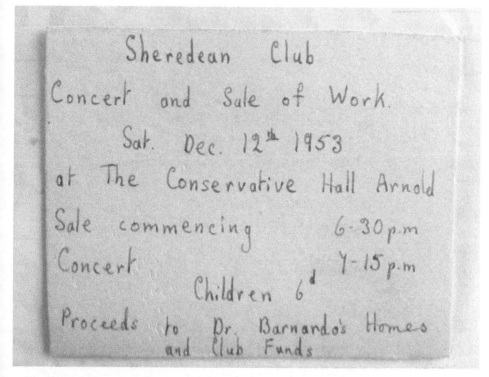

The Hand Written notice

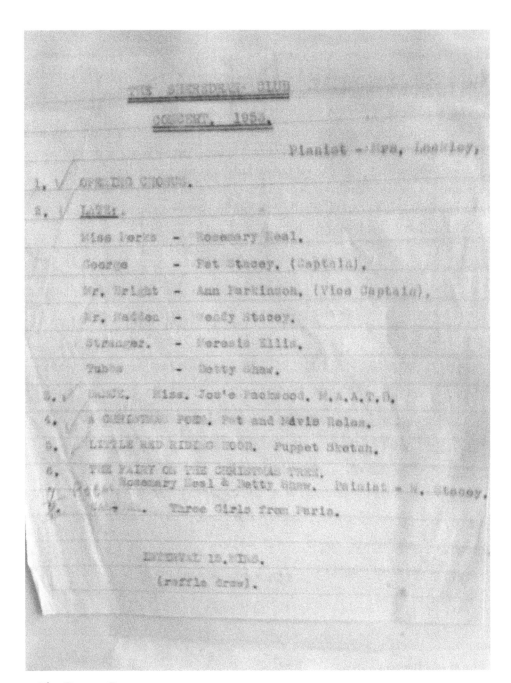

THE .... CLUB

CONCERT, 1954.

Pianist - Mrs. Loakley;

1. OPENING CHORUS.

2. LoVE.

Miss Perks   - Rosemary Neal.

George   - Pat Stacey, (Captain),

Mr. Wright   - Ann Parkinson, (Vice Captain),

Mr. Madden   - Wendy Stacey.

Stranger.   - Veronica Ellis.

Tubbs   - Betty Shaw.

3. DANCE.   Miss. Jou's Packwood, M.A.A.T.D.

4. A CHRISTMAS POEM. Pat and Mavis Roles.

5. LITTLE RED RIDING HOOD, Puppet Sketch.

6. THE FAIRY ON THE CHRISTMAS TREE.
     Rosemary Neal & Betty Shaw. Pianist - W. Stacey.

7. DANCES. Three Girls from Paris.

INTERVAL 10. MINS.

(raffle draw).

The Concert Programme

100

Money taken at Concert.			
Raffle	£2	2	6
Sale of Work	5	17	3½
Ticket Money	2	17	0
At Door		5	6
in the bucket			7
Treasure Hunt		7	11
Blanket	1	11	6
	13	2	3½

Money taken at the Concert

The total money taken at the Concert and Sale of Work was £13-2-3½d, of course this was not all profit, as we had to pay for the Hall and prizes costing about £1 and things for the raffle, about £3.

But we were very pleased to be able to send to Dr Barnardo's Homes £5 as a result of our efforts and keeping the rest for Club funds. Here is the receipt.

The concert was on December 12th and the Senior Christmas Party on the 22nd and then on 24th of December we went Carol Singing.

The party was as usual a happy event, and I took the opportunity of thanking all the members for their wonderful display on the most successful Club Concert ever. Betty presented Mum and Dad with a Brass Shovel with Robin Hood on the handle, and we thanked them again for letting us meet at 'Sheredean'. The Club gave me a bottle of my favourite Hand Cream and two hankies as well, which was very nice of them. Rosemary Neal was in London at the time of the party, but we were pleased to have Rosemary Lockley with us, and Derek.

(I am noticing that the name Derek is starting to crop up, he was by this time Pat's Boy Friend, the story of their romance will appear in a later chapter MP)

We had plenty of eats and played games etcetera but the prizes and results of the year, were one of the main features of the evening.

Results as follows.

Points Winner - Wendy with 202 points.

Rosemary Neal was given a special prize having got 147 points.

Attendance - Wendy with 42 out of 43.

Cup winners - Rosemary Neal and Wendy with 3 times each.

And now follow Carol Singing receipt and Letter (Singing by Senior Club only).

I feel I must include Junior Club party and results in 1953 although it was not held until January 5th.

Points winner - Pat Roles with 75 points.

Attendance - Pat Roles and Mavis Roles 23 out of 23.

Vice Captain, Wendy and Rosemary came to help with the party, and Rosemary received her prizes then. The whole party was a great success. In fact the whole year, I think, was a real success in every way, and I hope the next will be as good.

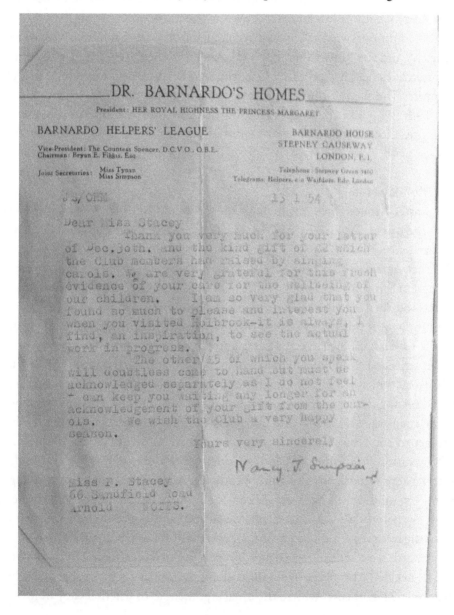

Sheredean Chapter 9

1954

Written by Pat Stacey, essays, Ann Parkinson, Joyce Parkinson, Meresia Ellis, Wendy Stacey and Rosemary Neal

OUR FIRST MEETING IN 1954 was Jan 12th and we were pleased to welcome back Joyce Parkinson who was a member in 1948 and 49. The committee picked were Cap, V. Cap, Wendy as Leader and Meresia as secretary.

Leader for Juniors was Pat Ellis and Second Pat Roles. The Club rules were revised in February and the Motto altered as well. And after these were learnt we had new green and gold shield badges with SC in Monogram, all made for us. On March the 9th Jennifer Thomas left the club because she was taking up music lessons, but on March 19th Peggy Lowton joined. Nothing had been planned for Easter, but at the last minute, Vice Captain decided to take the Seniors out on Easter Monday. Ann writes:-

Easter Monday Hike

On Easter Monday five members of the Club and one old member, went on a hike. They were, Wendy, Joyce, Meresia, Peggy, Myself and Gillian was the old member.

We met outside the Library at 10-45 and as we all arrived early we were in Huntingdon Street bus station soon after 11am. Gillian and Meresia went for a cup of coffee and then we all waited for the South Notts Bus which was to take us to Loughborough. It was in at 11-20 so we climbed aboard. The bus left at 11-30 and the route which it took enabled us to see quite a good bit of the Countryside on the way. We arrived at Loughborough just before 12-30 and started walking along the B5030 Road which led out of Loughborough and as we kept walking the scenery changed getting more and more countrified. I was the only one who knew just how long the road was (2¾ miles) and every few minutes I would be asked 'oh when do we get to the Cross Roads' of course we did arrive eventually and turned left past Nanpanton Post Office. We looked longingly at the reservoir but as it looked private we kept walking. By this time Wendy was rubbing her tummy and saying 'I want my egg sandwiches'. We were making for a stream that Captain and I had seen a few weeks before. We walked into one wood and came out to the Road. When we came to the stream we found a grassy spot and sat down and had our dinner.

Afterwards we all felt refreshed and Joyce stayed to look after the things and the rest of us decided to explore. We walked along the stream by the stones and when we reached a herd of cows we had the usual argument as to whether they were bulls or cows. When we were coming back through the field all the cows started walking towards us and we made a mad dash across the stream into the next field and started running, we were almost helpless with laughter when we realised the cows were going to the Farm to be milked.

After that we decided to walk through the fields back to Loughborough following a path to another stream and we finished what we had to eat and caught the 5-30 bus back home.

Ann Parkinson

On May 25th I cancelled the Juniors because of me starting a new job, and at Seniors we decided that Juniors would start at 6-15pm with the Leader and Second taking the first game and finish at 7-15pm and at 7-00pm the Seniors would start with Vice Captain taking the first game. However we cancelled the Juniors on June 1st so that we could have an evening out, which proved very successful and we wanted to go again. Joyce will tell you what we did.

Visit to Highfields, Nottingham

On June 1st 1954, Captain, Vice Captain, Betty, Meresia, Rosemary, Ann and myself met in Nottingham at 6-45pm and caught a Beeston Bus from which we alighted at Highfields. When we arrived Ann and Rosemary said that they wanted to go on the Lake in a boat but Captain said that they could when we had been for a walk first.

We walked along the side of the lake until we reached the paddling pool. There, Betty, Rosemary, Ann and myself took off our shoes and socks and started paddling. The water was very cold but we soon got used to it. Later, Captain decided to paddle with the rest of us.

After a quarter of an hour we dried ourselves and had a few races round the pond to get warm. When we were warm we all set off back to the boating lake. When we arrived there, Betty and myself didn't want to go on a boat, but when the rest of them were on the water we decided that we would go on after all, so we hired a canoe.

We stayed on the water for half an hour, and when we came off we all looked rather wet, but we didn't mind. After that we had an ice cream each and then set off for the bus stop. We arrived home at about 9 o'clock, and we all agreed that we had enjoyed ourselves thoroughly.

J. Parkinson

On June 15th we gained a new Junior named Kathleen . The following week, June 22nd a new senior joined named Carol. We had a camp down the garden on Saturday 3rd July, with Gillian and Meresia in charge of food and Wendy in charge of wood.

Camping down the Garden

On Saturday most of the club decided to camp down the garden, luckily we chose a fine weekend, and after some struggles we managed to get the Bell Tent up, Pat and I ran in with the tent-pole, and so got out of the hard work of putting the tent pegs in with the mallets, one of the head's kept flying off every so often, and much to everyone's concern and disgust, it did not hit anyone.

Gillian and I had a small lightweight tent, and after a hot drink we went to bed and started to eat and drink again, and we invited Derek Briggs in to share it. Also we had a big bag of 'Lemonade Powder', which somehow we kept spilling in our bed, very uncomfortable!!!

In the morning Gillian and I cooked breakfast and even Wendy enjoyed it so it must have been good. After this we took the tents down, cleared up and some of them went a walk, so I suppose someone else will have to say something of this.

Meresia

Our walk took us up Gedling Lane, along the plains and down the fields, not very far but enjoyable.

After this weekend, we talked of nothing but camp, at all the Tuesday night meetings. At the last meeting we still didn't know where we were going, or how we should get there, but get there we most certainly would. And so I kept trying. In August Vice Captain and I took the Juniors to Newstead Abbey for their outing.

Junior outing to Newstead Abbey August 1954

In August 1954, Captain and myself set out with the Junior Club for their outing to Newstead Abbey. It was rather dull when we boarded the bus at Huntingdon Street and as the bus set off there was a real downpour. It had stopped by the time we got to Newstead Abbey Gates and we had just enough time to walk down the drive before there was another. We sheltered until it was fine once again and then set off to see the Waterfall. Mavis managed to slip over in the mud that we had to cross to get to the Waterfall. After that we had a paddle and took some snaps. We then went for a short walk and sat down by a pond to eat our tea.

By this time the sun had come out and it was quite warm. We went to the Eagle Pond which was near to the Abbey itself and Pat and Janet did an exhibition of dancing for us. We then walked slowly up the drive and caught a bus home. (Photos over the page).

A Parkinson VC

Junior outing to Newstead Abbey

The Eagle Pond at Newstead Abbey under the left one and Pat Roles and Janet dancing at Newstead under the right one

We did not get the final arrangements made for camp, until the weekend before we went, Daddy took me down to see the site at Dunwich, in Suffolk, which we had had offered to us, and to see if we could arrange some transport at that end, which we did quite successfully, after all the worrying etcetera.

We have some lovely photos to put in, and I think some of us would like to write a piece in this log book, of what seemed to be the best camp ever.

Dunwich camp 1954

Seven of us were intending camping that week, they being Cap, Vice Cap, Wendy, Gillian, Joyce, Peggy and Margaret. As Mr and Mrs Stacey were intending to take a week of their holiday on that coast they took Peggy and Gillian with them in the car.

Sunday, a tiring day of travelling

The train which we were to catch to take us to London was due to leave Nottingham Midland Station at 6am, so those travelling by train were up at the crack of dawn. We all caught the train in good time and as the train was fast and only made three stops on the way, we were soon in London. Then followed an amusing time, that of crossing London by the Underground, (some of them had baggage as large as themselves). We were soon on the train which was to take us to Saxmundham, the station nearest to Dunwich.

The journey was soon over and we found Mr and Mrs Stacey, Peggy and Gillian waiting for us. The Coastguard came with his furniture lorry to take us on the last lap to the edge of England. It really was a bumpy ride, as we enjoyed it, we were all eager to catch a glimpse of the sea and we were very thrilled to see the lovely Heather and we were pleased to discover, later on, that we were actually camping on it.

Yes, it was a lovely site. We were told so by Cap, after she had been on the visit, but we all wanted to see for ourselves. We chose our place to camp, it was not on the very edge of the cliff but nearer the rough track, down which we had come in the Van. We pitched our tents and then started war on our sandwiches which were soon eaten. By this time it was getting late and the sun was beginning to disappear and so after a little exploring we curled up in our sleeping bags and fell asleep.

Monday very wet indeed

When we awoke we were sorry to discover that it was raining quite hard. We dressed and had breakfast and did our camp duties and as it was about 1½ miles to the village and we hadn't much food at all, we prepared ourselves for the 'Long Trek' and this in the pouring rain. There was only one general store in Dunwich and I think the lady behind the counter must have thought there was an invasion when seven very wet people trooped in to buy as many stores as we could carry, to say nothing of the sweets and chocolates that were purchased. We returned home and cooked the Dinner and afterwards just messed around the camp as it was too wet to do much else. After tea the rest decided to go to bed early so Cap and I went for a walk along the beach and we really did enjoy ourselves with skimming stones and dodging waves.

Tuesday still wet - though very interesting
In the morning we got out of bed and saw that the sun was shining. The cooks, Peggy and Gillian, cooked the breakfast whilst Wendy, Margaret and I collected wood. After breakfast we decided that we would walk across the beach to Southwold. It is 4 miles to Walberswick and a short walk from there to the Ferry. Gillian and Peggy made the sandwiches while the rest of us made gadgets. At about 10-30am it started to rain and later on Mr and Mrs Stacey came up in the car, and on hearing our plans for the day said they would take us down to the village. When we were ready some of us went down in the car and waited for the second lot to come down. After buying various things and talking to the shop-keeper Mr and Mrs Stacey came down with the others. By now the rain was heavier but nevertheless we set off across the beach. Some of us were dodging the sea and soon got very wet. We reached Walberswick at 12-30 and sat on a seat and ate our lunch. While we were eating a duck came towards us and a man came to fetch him on a bicycle. By this time the rain had stopped.

After lunch we walked through Walberswick and eventually found the ferry. When we asked the ferry man about going across he said something that we could not understand because of his Suffolk dialect. We got on the boat and arrived at the other side safely although we thought he was going to tip us in. For this journey we were charged 2d each. When we had given him the money we started walking to the centre of Southwold which was 1½ miles. When we at last arrived there we split up to do our shopping, but we bumped into each other a number of times. In one shop Pat saw a deer stalking hat which she would have liked to buy for Mr Stacey. When all the shopping was done we went to the arranged meeting place at 5-00pm, and found out that a fish and chip shop would be open at 7-00pm, so we killed time by going to the amusement park at the end of the pier, where we nearly laughed the roof off playing various games. When we came out of there we went to the chip shop and ordered fish and chips for seven. Gillian said that she felt sick with all the fruit she had eaten but still had her fish and chips. In there we met some men who guessed that we came from Notts. On finishing we went out to try to find the bus to Dunwich. This we did with some success after waiting for about a half hour. It had started raining again now and when we arrived back at camp we found the 'Lats' and the 'Fire Shelter' were down. We did not bother about that at 9-30 at night so we went and curled up in our sleeping bags. Although the ground was dampened by the rain our spirits weren't.

J. Parkinson

Wednesday a real scorcher

When we awoke the sun was streaming in through the tent, it was really hot, and we were very exited to think it had turned fine, we were soon out and about, doing our work very willingly. The first thing I did was to fix up a clothes line, to dry the wet Macs' we were very lucky to find some old air-raid shelters quite near, and we had strung a line inside one of these, it had got the wet things out of the way, but had not dried them very much, however we soon had them dry on the line. We were busy all the morning, doing Camp duties, and cooking stew and steamed pudding for dinner.

As soon as rest hour was over we went down to one of the Cliff lookout posts, where we changed into our bathing things, we left our clothes there and ran down the sandy cliffs into the sea, we were soon in and enjoying ourselves, all except Joyce who had forgotten her costume, we stayed there all the afternoon, and when we went to dress, we had some trouble getting dry, as some boys kept watching us, however we were soon on camp preparing tea. After tea Ann and I left the others building castles on the sands and went for a walk into the village. It was a lovely evening.

Thursday

In the morning we quickly got tidied up, and made sandwiches, and took them with us, when we went hiking, we didn't go very far, before we were sun bathing, and very soon eating dinner, we had taken our bathing things with us, but on returning decided to change on camp, and were again soon in the sea, for most of the afternoon. Ann and I again walked to the village, we heard a terrific noise, coming from Mums hotel, we were told the next morning, that they had, had a 'do' on he lawn, dancing etcetera.

P. Stacey

Friday August 27th

This was the day for the Fancy Dress Parade. We woke up quite early and the sun was shining in through the tent flaps and as it was 'Wendy's team's' turn to do the cooking the rest of us stayed in our bags a little longer. After breakfast we carried on with our duties. During any spare time we tried to make our fancy dress

110

costumes. After dinner, potatoes and stew, we had our rest hour during which we played 'snakes and ladders' and a 'circus card game'. Actually these were presents for my sister. We then went swimming but the sea was full of horrid jelly-fish.

After this Gillian and myself went to the village via the beach, to the Beach Cafe. We saw Mr and Mrs Stacey with some friends, bathing. Mrs Stacey was sunburnt. On the way back we tried to walk along the cliffs all the way - impossible! We had to cut through some private grounds and we counted 13 dead rabbits. We made a song about them. It went to the tune of 'Ten Green Bottles' and worked the same. It was:-

One dead rabbit lying by the roadside.
One dead rabbit lying by the road.
And if one more rabbit should suddenly die.
There'd be two dead rabbits lying by the road.
(I think you readers can guess the rest going up to 10 MP)

After tea we met some boys and we shouted to them but they did not hear us but, as they were coming back by the camp we asked them to stay to our fancy-dress parade. Pat dressed as a mermaid with the silver ground sheet around her legs for a tail. Margaret dressed as Gillian, Joyce dressed as myself. Ann dressed as a self raising flour bag, while Gillian and myself dressed as Hawaiian Islanders, covered in cocoa stain, fern and heather, while sitting under a palm tree? Mr and Mrs Stacey came to see us and they brought some friends along with them. Ann won the first prize for being the most original. Gillian and myself won the second prize.

After getting changed and washing the cocoa from our body's we stood round the fire drinking cocoa. The boys sawed a log for us and then we had a friendly fight with the wood pile. It was not till midnight that they went home and Pat had to lend Gordon a lamp for his bike. They must have got home about 1 o'clock as some were on foot.

Saturday

Saturday was another scorcher, today we had to get ready for several things, Peggy and I hurried and finished our daily chores leaving the rest to cook dinner. We walked along the beach for about one mile to the nearest 'tuck shop and cafe' combined. With us we took a couple of 'ruck sacks' to fill them with tuck for our midnight feast. We went back along the sands pinching a few sweets from the sacks now and again.

After dinner we spent nearly all our time collecting wood, with the help of a couple of boys, for the camp fire we were having that night. The rest of the time we had to spare we spent bathing and eating and of course doing our daily chores.

Everything was set for the camp fire, the boys included, until some bright spark suggested a swim. So Pat, Peggy, Joyce and two of the boys had a quick dip, in and out, (waste of time if you ask me). About 7 o'clock we lit the fire, everything was quite calm at first (including the sea).

Later we seemed to be getting in the camp fire mood (warming up as one might say). Finally Pat found a suitor, Ann had a suitor and of course a suitor managed to find me. Pat and co and Ann and co and me and co went for walks managing to go in different ways, leaving Peggy, Wendy and Margaret and Joyce to look after the two boys that were left to look after the fire. Later in fact very later we all gathered together at the camp fire and made ourselves a cup of night cup 'Coco'. Our friends left us ½ passed the next day and of course not forgetting our ½ hour late midnight feast. In fact by the time we were asleep it was time to get up 'Captains Orders'.

Gillian Morris

(I do not fully understand parts of the last paragraph so will leave it to the readers imagination, perhaps there is deliberate miss spelling of a word. MP)

The Beach at Dunwich

Dunwich

Gill on the beach.

Gill in the beach

The Bathing Belles.

Ann and Richard

The Smashers

Under the Palm Tree.

Club Camp 1954.

The Camp Site   The Wood Pile.

The Hunters.   Gill.

Cap. and Gordon.   All the Campers.

114

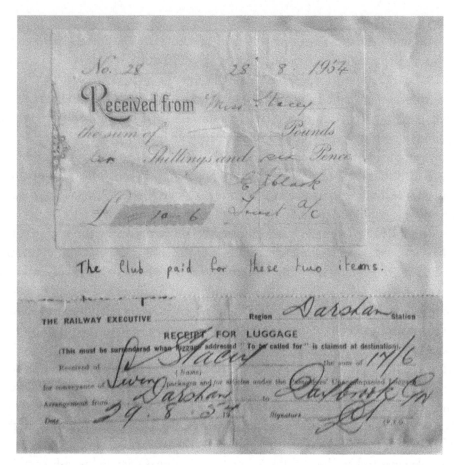

Receipts for the transit of luggage

We had no meetings during August but started afresh on September 7th and on September 21st a new member named Kathleen Millington joined us, but unfortunately Carol left us as she started a new school and wanted the time for home-work.

We were very sorry on October 19th to find that Betty Shaw was leaving us, after 4½ years in the Club, and the same night Kathleen left us, as she did not like the rules, and so was not enrolled as a member.

The following week the Club made me very happy by presenting me with a lovely lace tablecloth for my 21st birthday. I have put it in my bottom drawer. I shall take care of it, I shall always think of the grand set of girls who gave it to me, when I use it. By this time we were all well and truly on with the concert practices, we really did rack our brains to find something different, but we seemed to be so short of time and not getting on with the plays or songs well at all. The Junior play had to be cancelled altogether. But anyway we went through with the show. Wendy reports:-

Concert 1954

Our second Christmas concert was held on the 11th December 1954, at the Front Street Baptist Hall in Arnold, Nottingham. For the first time we had a stage, lights and a large room to serve as a dressing room.

In the afternoon we had a terrible dress rehearsal, especially the long play, when we spilt paraffin over Mummy's green curtains, and the fish and shrimps which Peggy had bought from Daybrook Fisheries smelt awful!

However the evening came at last and we got ready for the Sale of Work. People began to arrive about 7 o'clock and half an hour later we sang our usual opening chorus, after which five of us acted (or tried to act) 'Old Moores Almanac', a comedy which we were supposed to be doing for the first time that night.

Ann Junior played a piano solo, followed by short poems by the Junior Club, and then José, who had become engaged before the show and was our guest artist danced to us very gracefully. This was followed by 'McNamara's Band', rather a difference as we made as much noise as possible with tin pipes and saucepan lids.

Next Rosemary and Margaret sang 'Tea for Two', accompanied by Mrs Lockley at the piano and Joyce said 'The Little Mischief'. After a song by Ann Junior; Vice Cap and Gillian acted 'Wedding Bells' excellently.

After the interval, during which raffle tickets were sold, came the longest play 'The Bugginse's Picnic' (which we all thought would be the biggest flop of the show, judging by the dress rehearsal). However it went off quite well after all, although there was a bit more fun when I produced a sardine tin, saying 'You might open this tin of SALMON!!! WE also missed a bit out, but luckily nobody noticed except us'.

This play was to have been followed by Cap singing 'O My Beloved Father' but very unfortunately, she had a bad cold and so could not do so. Meresia then said a poem, and my piano solo was followed by Gillian's poem and another dance by José. Janet from the Juniors said three little poems and Pat Ellis sang a Carol. My poem was then followed by several songs by all of us. Gillian particularly, did very well in 'Dry Bones' with Peggy, Rosemary and Joyce as dancers.

The concert ended with the usual chorus and then we heaved a sigh of relief when all was over. We had all, however, enjoyed ourselves thoroughly (as usual) and hope all who supported us did too.

Wendy

Yes, we certainly enjoyed doing the show, and I was most disappointed that I couldn't sing, however I am sure it was a success. Programme over next page.

THE SHERRDEAT CLUB CONCERT 1954

Pianist.-Mrs Lockle

1. Opening Chorus.
2. Old Moore's Almanac.

   Lady Ditchwater.   Meresia Ellis.
   Sir John   "   Pat Stacey. (Captain).
   Algernon   "   Joyce Parkinson.
   Daisy Dimple.   Wendy Stacey.
   Evelyn Teat.   Rosemary Neal.
3. Piano Solo.   Ann Taylor.
4. Poems.   Junior Club.
5. Dance.   Jos's Backwood. M.A.A.C.D.
6. Macnama's   Senior Club.
7. The Band.   "   "
8. Tea for for two.   Rosemary Neal and Margaret Witt.
9. Poem.   Joyce Parkinson.
10. Cruising Down the River.   Ann Taylor.
11. Poem.   Rosemary Neal.
12. Wedding Bells. Bride   Ann Parkinson.(Vice Capt La)
    Bridesmaid   Gillian Morris.
                    INTERVAL.
13. The Bugginse's Fiddle.
    Mrs. Buggins   Wendy Stacey.
    Father   "   Peggy Lowton.
    Grandma "   Ann Parkinson.(Vice Captain)
    Anne   "   Rosemary Neal.
    Alfie   "   Ann Taylor.
14. Oh, my Beloved Father   Pat Stacey (Captain.)
15. Poem   Meresia Ellis.
16. Piano Solo   Wendy Stacey.
17. Gillian Poem   Gillian Morris.
18. Dance   Jos's Backwood. M.A.A.C.
19. Three Rhymes   Janet Athey.
20. Song.   Pat Ellis.
21. Poem   Wendy Stacey.
22. Songs.   All Club.
23. Ending Chorus.

The Concert Programme

117

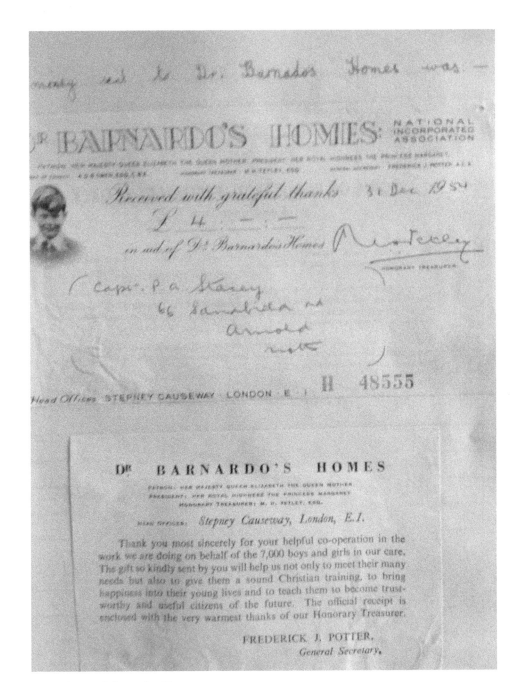

£4 donated from the Concert

The Xmas party was the Tuesday before Christmas as usual, and we had tea first followed by the prize giving, and games.

The results were as follows:-

Attendance - Seniors - Rosemary Neal - 42 out of 42
Attendance -Juniors - Pat Ellis and Mavis Roles - 39 out of 39
Points -Seniors - Wendy Stacey - 167
Points - Juniors - Pat Roles -141
Cup winners - Wendy Stacey and Peggy Lowton
Silver Milk Tops - Pat Ellis - 3,179 tops

Mum and Dad had their presents given by one of the Club - Mum, Stockings and Dad, Tobacco. The Club gave me a bottle of Yardley's hand cream and two hankies.

Rosemary will now report on the 1954 Carol singing effort; following that I shall put in the receipt and letter from Dr Barnardo's Homes.

We started Carol singing at 7 o'clock on the night before Christmas Eve. It was really cold. The first place we went to was Mrs Read, as we entered her gate we were informed by some boys that we wouldn't get anything from her. Anyway we started singing and when we had finished she came to the door and said 'Have you been Carol Singing?' she hadn't heard us. After that we went to call on Meresia, then we went to Mrs Stacy Blakes, as we had got half way through the verse, she opened the door and said 'is it the Sheredean Club?' and we said 'yes', she made us go in and sing in the hall without a light on. Pat, her daughter went and opened the door of her Father's bedroom as he wasn't very well. When we had done she gave us mince pies. We went to various other places and finished up having tea and biscuits at Mrs Briggs.

Captain (written for Rosemary Neal)

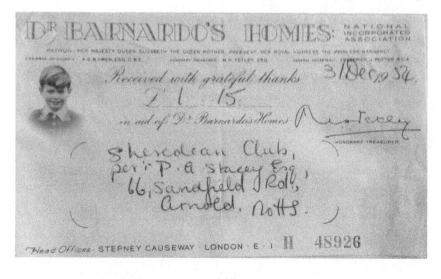

119

BARNARDO-DAY FUND

Chairman: BRYAN E. FIGGIS, Esq.
Secretary: ANEURIN JONES, B.A.

Telegrams: JONES, WAPLONA, ESQ. LONDON
Telephone: STEPNEY GREEN 3401

Head Office: 18-26 STEPNEY CAUSEWAY,
LONDON, E.1.

AJ/BW

11th January, 1965.

F. A. Stacey Esq.,
66, Sandfield Road,
Arnold, Notts.

Dear Mr. Stacey,

It is with deep gratitude I acknowledge receipt of your welcome gift of £1. 15s. 0d. being the proceeds of the Carol Singing Effort you so kindly arranged on our behalf. I have pleasure in enclosing our Honorary Treasurer's receipt and I shall be glad if you will accept for yourself and convey to the Members of your Carol Party my very warm thanks.

I do hope your own joy will be greatly increased as you think of the happiness your kindness has brought to some of our boys and girls.

With all good wishes,

Yours sincerely,

aneurin jones

120

Sheredean Chapter 10

1955

Written by Pat Stacey, essays, Pat Stacey, Joyce Parkinson, Wendy Stacey and Patricia Ellis

WE WERE MORE THAN PLEASED to welcome back Gillian as a full member again. The committee chosen were as last year:-

Leader - Wendy, Sec - Meresia, with the addition of Gillian. The Junior Club chose Pat Ellis as Leader and Kathleen as second, Kathleen left the club so Pat Roles took over her place as second.

We had two long committee meetings with some very ambitious ideas. In February I sent off to Elton, Hartington and Ilam Youth Hostels for our Easter hiking expedition, Good Friday to Easter Tuesday. We decided that there would be no camp this year, but we would save up for a 1956 camp.

All those who went hosteling at Easter had to join the Youth Hostel Organisation as I could not get a permit on a bank holiday. Here we have some reports of the trip and photo's taken while there:-

50 Miles in 5 days

On Good Friday early in the morning we set off to catch the 7-55am bus from Huntington Street. We being Wendy, Joyce, Peggy, Rosemary and myself, we had quite a rush but caught it alright. We went by bus to Matlock and then we started walking, first of all we went up a very steep hill out of Matlock, and then across some fields. We were walking along by the hedge, when quite suddenly we saw Peggy had caught a budgie, a very pretty bird, she had just picked hold of it, as it sat in the hedge. We cold see a farm only a short distance away so we called there to see if they had lost one. They hadn't but told Peggy and Wendy who had. While we waited on the road side they went back to Matlock with the bird. However they couldn't find the right owner, but a gentleman gave them 5 shillings for the bird and they left it with him, he said 'he would keep it if no one claimed it, as he had lost his own budgie'.

After this we carried on over Oker Hill and down to Darley Bridge and climbed up quite high again before having dinner, after dinner we went to Birchover and then to Elton Youth Hostel via Dudwood Farm.

Elton is a self cooking only Hostel and we were soon busy, cooking our supper. After this we played cards and dominoes before going to bed. Next morning we cooked breakfast, and did our duties, this took some time as the Warden was very strict on the blankets being folded correctly, and she kept coming to inspect them.

When we eventually made a start, we made for Winster where we met Gillian and Meresia, after this we went back through Elton across to Dale End and Lowfield Farm, it was here that we made friends with the lamb, which Gill is holding in the photo, it kept following us, so Gill took it into another field where we hoped it would find it's Mum.

After this we got ourselves lost, we were making for Middleton, but there was no visible path; we went by the signpost when we reached a road, however we think the signpost was wrong, as we walked about a mile in the wrong direction. After asking, we found Rake Lane and Green Lane, it was a very pleasant walk along these lanes to Hartington.

After a very welcome supper we played cards on the common room floor, and a man played the piano while we sang, he called us "The Choir', his signature tune was 'The Happy Wanderer' which he played over a dozen times, much to everyones amusement.

The next day (Sunday) we walked from Hartington to Ilam through the dales, it rained at the beginning of the journey. The River was very high and the path extremely muddy. Our song of the day was Mud, Mud, glorious Mud.

A man hunted us all day, and he wouldn't go anywhere without me, and we had to share all our food and everything with him. He was alright but we couldn't shake him off, and we had a real laugh when some of us climbed Thorpe Cloud he went with us and held Meresia's hand all the way up and down the other side, he saw her climbing on her hands and knees, and he said 'Oh no, we can't have this' and took over from there. By the way, the stepping stones were covered with water; I also should have put that we visited the Hermits Cave, yesterday, near Elton, where some of the photos were taken.

We arrived at the hostel before five and had to wait in the queue. Our man friend hadn't booked but managed to get in, he sat with us throughout supper, but after this we started dancing and finally got rid of him. I danced with two scout masters, one tall and thin, the other one short and bald, they were both very nice, and we asked them to arrange a camp fire sing song for the last ½ hour of the evening, which they did; the night before, they told us, there had been lots of scouts and they had had a real good sing song.

We didn't see Gill during camp fire, as she had been locked outside with a boy named Dave. I saw her just after the warden had let them in, and told them off.

Monday morning our friend took our photo with our camera and also took a snap of us with his own camera, some weeks after he wrote to me and sent a coloured Photo of us all, of course we were very thrilled with this. However we made sure we were going in the opposite direction to him. Our route took us through the grounds of Ilam Hall, over the river Manifold to Rushley, then up the hill by a track to

Throwley Hall. We spent some time here, watching two farmers and a small boy trying to catch a sheep, and trying also to stop it getting near the other sheep and lambs.They were trying to coax it with a dead lamb on the end of a rope. We weren't near enough to ask if we could help, so we kept the other side of the wall so as not to do the wrong thing. Eventually they got it cornered, and we were able to continue our walk to Oldpark Hill, and then we went about 1½ miles out of our way to climb up to Thors Cave (1000 feet above sea level) and to get a drink from Wetton Mill cafe in the Manifold Valley. We retraced our steps and continued along the foot-path (which used to be a railway track) along the River Hamps to Greensides (near Waterhouses) it was a long and tiring walk and we crossed about 13 small bridges along the path. Then we took the road to Carlton and back through Rushley and to Ilam Hall, about 15 miles altogether.

We were about all in when we arrived and were pleased to be shown a quicker way into the Hostel; although some of the girls were suffering from blisters, I'm pleased to say we didn't hear much in the way of grumbles.

Pat Stacey

Monday Night

On Monday night Gillian and Meresia left us because they had to go to work the following day.

When we reached Ilam Hostel the first thing we did was to have a very good wash . We didn't have to make our beds because that was the second night there and we had already made them. After changing our clothes we went downstairs into the common room (dining room also) where we started talking to some people who were there.

At about 6-30pm the warden came in to put chairs and tables up for dinner, so we helped him. At 7pm we had dinner which was very appetising.

After dinner we retired to the library and then asked the warden if we could dance as we had done the previous night. He said we could and he fetched the gram-ophone and took it to the common room. Soon after, dancing was in full swing. It was about 10-45pm when the warden came and told us to pack up. The next morning we didn't wake up till 7am.

Tuesday

On Tuesday morning we had breakfast and then went to get our packs ready to depart. That finished, we went to find what our duty was to be then we fetched our cards and prepared to leave.

First of all we went to Dovedale and all the girls except myself climbed Thorpe Cloud while I stayed to look after the packs. When they came down we began to walk by the river to some remote village called Mapleton where we had a very refreshing drink. Before we had reached the village we had stopped to have some dinner. After the drinks we made our way across some fields until we reached a stream where we had a paddle. When we were ready, we set off again and our next stop was Ashbourne. We did just manage to miss a bus owing to Pat going for some coffee. We didn't think we would get another bus for another hour but a 'duplicate' came, so we boarded it and clambered to the back of the bus. This bus took us to Derby.

From Derby we caught a bus to Nottingham and then on to our homes. We arrived home at about 5pm. We all agreed that we had enjoyed ourselves thoroughly despite blisters, scratches, and aches of all kinds.

J. Parkinson

Taken near Hermits cave – Elton.

Gill is holding the lamb, top left

This is the slide from the envelope

In April Janet left the Junior club and so that made only 4 Juniors. On May 3rd Vice Captain took the Juniors while Gillian and I set off for Huckerby's Farm on our bikes. The others came with Vice Cap under sealed orders and tracking signs, when they arrived Gill and I had a lovely fire going and the Kettle boiling, we all had tea or coco and then we put the fire out, and set off for home, four of us walked along Mapperley and arrived home about 9-30pm. Gill and Ann went back by bike, V Cap and Joyce walked back through Arnold and Margaret and Peggy went by the fields and got chased by a cow!!

I am sure we all enjoyed ourselves despite the wind and rain, and we came home feeling happy but rather dirty. In fairness I should add the Farmers wife gave us warm water to start the kettle boiling.

At our next meeting, it rained and we were busy working on baskets etcetera, Gillian kidded Peggy on that she was engaged to Dave. (She was wearing my dress ring) what a laugh we had after Peggy and the Club had gone.

June the 14th Jacqueline joined the Club but left again in September owing to homework. On June 21st Pat Leverton joined us. We had a lovely summer and were able to play many outdoor games, cricket, rounders, tracking and stalking etc.

As the summer drew to a close and the darker evenings came we started practising for the Concert. This we soon got going in full swing, we really did work hard, and most of us worked very hard for the Sale of Work. Those doing a great deal for the sale were Joyce, Peggy and Gillian, and I would like to thank them very much for the effort, also to Wendy for doing the typing, I could and should mention all the things the girls have done, but I will stop here saying, thank you to them all, for working so well with me.

P. Stacey

Concert 1955

On December 11th, the night before our concert was due to be put on at the Front Street Baptist Hall, a few of us went down to look at the stage to see what needed to be done the following day.

On Saturday morning Penny, Gill, Pat Ellis and myself had a very bumpy but enjoyable ride down Langley Avenue on one of Mr Hills' lorries with all the props.

We then got cracking with various odd curtains, dozens of pins and yards of sellotape, and made the stage and stall for the sale of work look a bit more presentable, and pinned bamboo canes on a piece of curtain for the Hawaiian Scene. We had a dress rehearsal in the afternoon and Mrs Lockley very kindly came down to play the piano for us. I'll say nothing more about that afternoon, but leave it to your imagination!

The evening started at 7-15pm, after the sale of work, with a play 'Mr Hackets

Alibi. It was quite an event for us when Peggy (Mr Hackett) actually did drop the clock, instead of allowing a piece of paper to float slowly and silently to the floor, as at rehearsals, which did not give quite the same effect, needless to say!

José danced twice for us during the evening and, at the end of the first half, the Seniors put on a Hawaiian Scene with grass skirts and flower garlands, with which José had helped - to try make us do a few dancing steps. (I was 16 and operated the curtains for this concert, see Chapter 1 MP)

After a short interval, during which raffle tickets were sold, three other seniors, Vice Cap, Gill, and Rosemary - performed another play 'Fame'. Cap and Vice Cap, later did 'Back over the years' in which they spoke about our various activities during the past ten years. Also Cap and I did a Puppet Show, in which Meresia and Vic Cap spoke the voices of the characters in 'Alice in Wonderland'.

The evening drew to a close very successfully with a number of Christmas Songs in which all the Club joined.

When we went back into the dressing room there was the usual mess to clear up, but we all agreed that we had enjoyed the show, although we were thankful it was all over.

Wendy

A picture sent by Dr Barnardo's Homes

PROGRAME.

Play   Mr. Hackett's Alibi. Wendy, Joyce, Margaret, Peggy,
                                                (Prompt Gillian

Piano   Ann Taylor.

Oh My Beloved Fahher.   Captain.

What Child is This Wendy & Margaret.

Dance   Jose.

Lullaby.   Pat Ellis.

Hawiian Songs   Seniors.   - Solo's - Wendy.

        INTERVAL.   15 Mins.

Play Fame.   V.C. Gillian, Rosemary.   Prompt Joyce.

Piano   Wendy.

The Indian Love Call Captain.

Back over the Years.   Cap. & V.C.,
A Show Piece by Ann Taylor.
Piano   Margaret.

Alice in Wonderland Captain, V.C., Wendy, Meresia.

The Little Old Mill.   Ann Taylor.

Dance   Jose.

Christmas Songs.   All.,

Vote of Thanks.   Captain.

THE QUEEN.

Part of the typed programme

128

SHEREDEAN CLUB

Admission :
Adults 1/6
Children 9d.

Concert
AND SALE OF WORK
Saturday, Dec. 10th, 1955

At Front Street Baptist School Hall

Commencing with Sale of Work at 7.0 p.m.

A printed notice

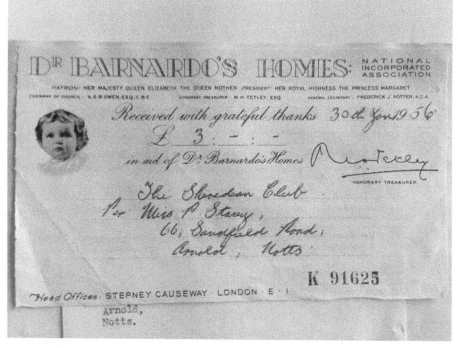

Receipt for £3 donation

DR. BARNARDO'S HOMES : NATIONAL INCORPORATED ASSOCIATION.

From
FREDERICK J. POTTER, A.C.A.   FJP/D/PH.
General Secretary.

HEAD OFFICES:
STEPNEY CAUSEWAY,
LONDON, E.1.

31st January, 1956.

Miss E. Stacey,
66, Sandfield Road,
Arnold,
Notts.

Dear Miss Stacey,

We send our warmest thanks for all the members
of the Sheredean Club for the great work that you
have done on behalf of our boys and girls. You
are to be congratulated on raising such a fine
total through your Annual Concert, which must
have been a great success and we send to you all
our warm thanks for the £3 which has been allotted
to us as a share of the profits you made. It is a
great encouragement to us to have such good friends
and we would like you all to know how much
your interest is appreciated.

I venture to enclose a complimentary copy of
our 1956 calendar, which I hope you will accept
as a reminder of the great family you have helped
so much.

With every good wish,

Yours sincerely,

General Secretary.

Thank you letter

The receipt below, was the result of some very hard work by Penny Hill, and we didn't know anything about it until she presented us with 27 shillings to be sent to Dr Barnardo's. She and her 2 cousins had had a sale in their garden, selling cakes and drinks, things they had made, and charging for a go on the swing, and other side shows. I think they did very well indeed; Thanks Penny.

Captain

Receipt for 27shillings, actually £1-7

Christmas Party

As we had so many members in the club we decided to have the Christmas Party at the Baptist Hall. We arrived there at 7-0pm with our contributions for the tea. The table was set up and it really looked very nice. We invited Mr and Mrs Stacey and Michael Parkinson to the party. After we had cleared away the tea things we sat in a ring and played musical parcel. Then the prizes were given. The winners were:-

Wendy - 1st - with 35 out of 37 attendances and 25 stars.

Joyce (me) - 2nd - with 35 out of 37 attendances and 23 stars.

The Junior winners were:-

Pat Roles - Attendance

Pat Ellis - silver milk tops

After the prizes were given a small gift was presented to us all, then Rosemary presented Mrs Stacey with a pair of nylons and Mr Stacey some tobacco.

When this was finished we played games and when the Juniors had gone home we had some dancing. It was then time to pack up our things and go home. The idea of using the Hall seemed a very good one indeed, and I think all of us enjoyed ourselves.

J. Parkinson

Carol Singing

On Friday December 23rd the club went carol singing, there was Captain, Rosemary, Meresia, Wendy and Pat. We went to call for Ann Taylor and then went to meet Joyce, Peggy, and Pat Leverton at the 52 bus terminus. Soon after that we went to Peggy's house where we sang three songs. After that we went to several friends and relatives of Joyce's and Peggy's. We then went to Joyces house and sang, they asked us if we would like a mince pie and a cup of tea which we had. After eating and drinking, we called on some more friends of the seniors after that, we then went to Margarets home and saw that she didn't look very well. We went to Shiela Headleys and Shirley Marshalls. At about 9 o'clock we took Ann Taylor home but first we went to a boys house, we were in the middle of our first song when we felt a bucket of water being thrown over us. We didn't wait for more but moved quickly away. Meresia got most of the water, she was soaked. We went to dry off at Anns. We had a cup of tea and some biscuits which Mrs Taylor gave to us. We thought it would be about time to go home so we left Ann at her house, and made our way home.

Patricia R. Ellis

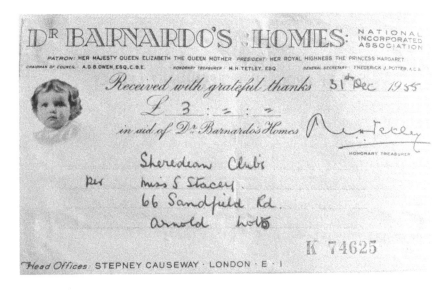

Letter from Dr Barnardo's but the Club did not tell them about the bucket of water

Rosemary Neal had to say goodbye to the Club as she has moved to Gorleston-on-Sea in Norfolk. She hopes to come and see us one day and maybe we shall go and see her, perhaps camping!

Sheredean Chapter 11

1956

Written by Pat Stacey, essays, Joyce Parkinson, Penny Hill, Pat Roles and Mavis Roles

OUR FIRST MEETING WAS JAN 10th we were all present except Mavis Roles who was ill, and Pat Leverton. The elections for the committee proceeded, and all last years committee members were re-elected. We had just the normal run of meetings in the house until the end of April, when we started having some outdoor games.

We had a letter from Pat Leverton during April, saying, 'that she wouldn't be coming anymore, as she was too busy'. We were sorry but not surprised to get this news, as she hadn't been to the Club since Jan 24th, and she was never enrolled as a member, as she was so often absent. However the excitement was growing during April as we were getting ourselves prepared to go Youth Hostelling on May 5th. We were learning the Hostel rules, the country code and making lists of what we should need. On May 1st all the last minute arrangements were seen to. All was ready for our Club outing to Rudyard Lake, near Leek, Cheshire, on May 5th. Joyce describes the first day.

The whole Club met at Mount Street Bus Station and caught the 1-55pm bus to Derby. From there we caught a bus to Leek, and when we alighted we started walking to the hostel. We had only about 3 miles to walk, but the juniors soon tired, owing to the fact that they had been dashing about playing games.

Arriving at the Youth Hostel we changed our shoes and made our beds. Having nothing else to do before supper we toured the grounds and went down to the Lake where some boys asked us to go in their boats. We decided against this as we wished to keep dry, and we didn't want to be late for supper. Had some of us, mainly the Juniors, not eaten so many sweets etcetera before supper, the supper would have been better appreciated. Our duty was washing up which we did after supper.

Meresia, Ann (V.C.), and Gillian went down to the village at Rudyard in the evening while the rest of us went into the common room to sing camp songs.

J.Parkinson

Rudyard Lake - Sunday

On Sunday morning every-body except Gillian were up and dressed before the rising bell. When we were ready we went for a walk, as it was not quite time for breakfast.

For breakfast we had porridge and then had something fried. Joyce wasn't in for breakfast as she was with a boy called John. After this V. capt went to the warden to get Joyces duty, it was sweeping the dormitory. When we were ready to go we changed our shoes and got our packed dinners. V. capt, carried most of them, because she had the most room in her haversack. When we were outside capt took a photograph of us all. After the photo had been taken I remembered I had forgotten my Robin Hood book, so I went back to the common room, after lending it to Pat Roles it had been left. When I had put it in my bag we started out.

Capt, and some of the others were a bit behind as we walked along, we did not keep to the path, but walked on the edge of the Lake. We walked for quite a while and then sat on a wall to wait for the others. After a while we set out again, Ann and I were a little behind.

After a while we caught the others up, and were very surprised to see them going through a small gate where they had seen Captain and some of the others. Mavis was rather slow so we had to wait for her. When we were all down we walked for quite a while and then we saw a shop so we all went to sit down but some of us went and bought sweets.

Across the road was a little path leading to a fair ground, so we decided to have our dinner there. There we met some of the boys that we had met at the hostel. The dinner was apricot jam and cheese sandwiches with a piece of Dundee cake.

After dinner Captain and Wendy went to take photographs and came back after a while. We all sat down to have a rest, and then we saw some rowing boats, and capt asked if any of us wanted to go in one. Some of us went in one while others waited to see if the motor boats were going out. We waited for quite a while and then found out we could not go in them.

When all who were going in a boat were off, Capt and Meresia went for a walk while Pat, Mavis, Ann and I went to the amusement park. After a while we were all back and together we started back home. We walked for quite a way singing as we went along.

When we arrived at the bus station we got into the bus. We travelled for quite a while and at last reached Derby where we changed buses.

When the bus started off we, all sat down to have a rest. At last we arrived at the Arnold library where we all said 'Good-bye'.

Penny Hill

(Penny was one of the youngest members of the Club, her father had a building company and used his lorry to take the Club to some of their camping adventures. The family lived on Sandfield Road MP).

Leek

Joyce

Peggy.

Y. H.

All the Club 1956.

Joyce & Peggy.

Gill & Cap up tree. & Pat Roles

"Monkey's!"   Meresla.

On May 15th we spent our club evening fire lighting and cooking supper up at Athey's old farm, it was a lovely evening and we had some smashing fires, and some of us had some smashing suppers!! We all enjoyed the fun.

At August Bank Holiday four of the Club went to Arnside Youth Hostel, Ann, Joyce, Peggy and Captain.

I arranged a camp at Bridlington from August 11th to18th for the Guides and the Club. Peggy was the only Club member who went and the Club paid some of the expenses for her.

Some of the Club saw Rosemary Neal, when she visited Nottingham for a week at the end of August. We were all pleased to see her, and hope we shall see her again some time. On September the 18th we had a camp fire sing song and cocoa all round. This was Margaret Whitt's last night at the Club. After this we had our second Youth Hostel Association trip for 1956 when on September 22nd we visited Ravenstor Youth Hostel, Pat Roles reports.

Ravenstor Youth Hostel

On Saturday September 22nd Captain, Margaret, Peggy, Carol, Mavis, Pat and myself set off on a Y.H.A. trip. We caught the 11-20am bus from Huntington Street bus station to Bakewell. From there we had a five mile walk to the hostel. We walked through fields for some time following a river. Then we came out on to the road. Then we came to a steep hill, which we all thoroughly enjoyed climbing up. At the top we stopped for a rest and refreshments. Then we went down the other side of the hill and through some more fields.

We arrived at the hostel at about 5 o'clock. We made our beds and then set about to explore the hostel. Carol palled up with a girl called Susan and went with her to watch her father cutting down trees.

Ann, Peter, Gillian, Joyce and Wendy arrived just before supper. Luckily they were all in our dormitory, all that is except for Peter. For supper we had vegetable soup, meat pie, potatoes, carrots and stodge with custard. Then we went into the common room and sang songs.

At eight o'clock Carol, Mavis, Pat and myself went up to bed, and left the seniors to finish singing their camp songs. Up stairs we were just settling in bed when Pat and Carol decided they would do some singing. They dressed and went downstairs and sang outside the common room door, or, at least they said they did. They came up singing 'There's a Hole in my bucket' and we all joined in singing it, then we sang 'One man went to Mow'. The seniors came up at 11 o'clock and soon all was quiet.

We were all awake early in the next morning and went for a walk before breakfast. For breakfast we had porridge, scrambled egg, bacon, fried bread, baked beans and bread and marmalade. Our jobs that morning were to sweep and tidy up the dining room, polish a cupboard in there, polish all the wooden things in the hall, unmake the beds, wash two tea towels and sweep out the dormitory.

While we were all ready to go and waiting for Peggy (who had gone off with a boy) we had our photo's taken on the steps of the hostel. Peggy came back not long after, and we set off with some boys on bicycles, (the Swadlincote Wheelers) along a path by a river. We followed the river for some time and then came out on to the road. We then went into another field. After a while we sat down and had our lunch at a place near Monsal Dale. The lunch was a sandwich of fish paste, one of lettuce and one of fish paste and lettuce mixed together. After lunch Captain and Margaret climbed up 1,000 foot hill, when they were half way up Pat Ellis and Carol went up after them.

Soon after, when Captain, Margaret, Pat and Carol had come down we went on our way again. We followed the river for some time and then came out on to the road. We arrived at the bus stop at 5-29 and we had half an hour to wait for the bus to come. We arrived in Nottingham at about 7 o'clock. Then somebody suggested that we walked all the way home, but nobody was in favour so we caught a bus.

Pat Roles

All during October we collected old clothes etcetera, to make the Guy for our bonfire on November 5th,. The Juniors made the Guy on the 30th of October, we dressed him up in an old shirt, tie, trousers, mac, gloves and hat and I made a face for him, using some old make up, on a pale pink cloth.

Bonfire night came on a Monday, so not all the club could make it, but anyway Mavis Roles is going to report on it.

Bonfire Night

On the Saturday before bonfire night Pat Ellis and myself went to club to get the bonfire ready. We went to Pat Ellis's house to get the wood she had been collecting. We took it back to the club bonfire which was in Captains garden and with the stuff that Captain had got started building the bonfire. When we had done that we went to my house to get some cardboard boxes. Mr Hill had brought up some old pictures for the guide jumble sale. They were no good so we broke them up for the bonfire.

On Monday morning Pat Ellis, Captain, Pat, Trevor and myself were all the people who came on time. We lit the fire and lit one or two sparklers and fireworks. Mr and Mrs Stacey came up and Mrs Stacey did some gardening. Mr Stacey went back, I gave him a sparkler to light his way. After a bit Ann Parkinson came. Later Captain put some chestnuts on to roast. They were very nice and when they were done she put some potatoes on. While we were having the chestnuts Mrs Stacey brought us a cup of tea and some cake. Later, Gillian came, she brought some tiny sparklers. Then Mummy came to take Pat, Trevor and myself home. Captain gave us three a bit of a small potato. It was not very nice because it was not quite done. Then we went home but the others stopped until the potatoes were done.

Mavis Roles

After November 5th we got cracking on the social, we really were very busy these last few weeks before 'the big night'. I shall not say anything about it now as Joyce is going to write in, a full report.

Unfortunately Gillian and Meresia were both ill during December and unable to come to the social, although they did help before hand quite a lot.

Social Evening

The social was held this year in the Conservative Hall on December 15th. Most of the club were at the Hall during the afternoon either rehearsing the Nativity or trying to help.

The social began as usual, with a sale of work and a few other features. When everyone had arrived a game was organised, and later dancing was in progress. During the evening we did the Nativity and after that there was some community singing which was enjoyed by everyone. Captain sang 'The Laughing Song' and Ann Taylor and Pat Ellis sang 'Santa Natalia'.

Refreshments consisting of cakes, cobs and a cup of tea, were welcomed by all. By about 10pm the Juniors and parents and friends had gone, and the seniors stayed to clear up, and left at about 10-45 pm after a very enjoyable evening.

J. Parkinson

On the following Tuesday evening we had a little party at Club, when the prizes were given out. The results were as follows:-

Senior points and attendance - Wendy Stacey

Junior points and attendance - Pat Roles

My Mum and Pop came in for the prize giving, and we presented them with a Christmas box each. The Club gave me some bath cubes and talcum powder.

Captain

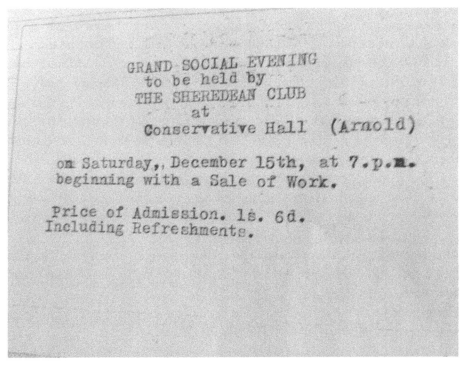

The typed notice for the Social Evening

Carol Singing

On Christmas Eve Captain, Pat Ellis, Wendy, Mavis, Judith, Betty, Rosemary Green, some friends of Wendy and myself went Carol Singing. We went down Sandfield Road first singing two or three Carols at the houses of people we knew. Then we came back up the other side of the road. At Mrs Briggs house we were given a sweet each, and Derek joined us. When we drew level with Mr and Mrs Stacey's house, we were all bitterly cold so we went inside for a drink and something to eat. After we were all warmed up we continued on up Sandfield Road. Then Mavis left us. Then we went to Mrs Blake's we were invited in and given a biscuit each. I then went home, but the rest of them went down to Betty's. At the end we had collected about £2.

Pat Roles

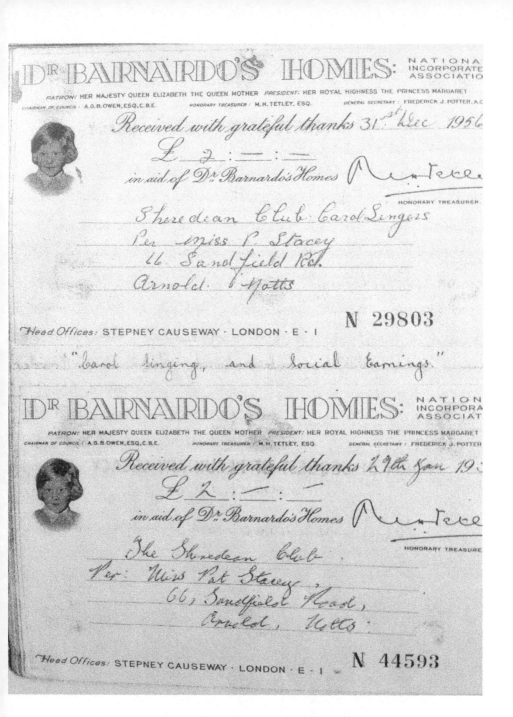

DR BARNARDO'S HOMES: NATIONAL INCORPORATE ASSOCIATIO

PATRON: HER MAJESTY QUEEN ELIZABETH THE QUEEN MOTHER PRESIDENT: HER ROYAL HIGHNESS THE PRINCESS MARGARET

CHAIRMAN OF COUNCIL · A.G.B.OWEN, ESQ. C.B.E.   HONORARY TREASURER · M.H.TETLEY, ESQ.   GENERAL SECRETARY · FREDERICK J. POTTER, A.C

Received with grateful thanks 31st Dec 1956

£ 2 : — : —

in aid of Dr Barnardo's Homes

HONORARY TREASURER.

Sheredean Club Carol Singers
Per Miss P. Stacey
66 Sandfield Rd.
Arnold · Notts

N 29803

Head Offices: STEPNEY CAUSEWAY · LONDON · E · I

"Carol Singing, and Social Earnings."

DR BARNARDO'S HOMES: NATION INCORPORA ASSOCIAT

PATRON: HER MAJESTY QUEEN ELIZABETH THE QUEEN MOTHER PRESIDENT: HER ROYAL HIGHNESS THE PRINCESS MARGARET

CHAIRMAN OF COUNCIL · A.G.B.OWEN, ESQ. C.B.E.   HONORARY TREASURER · M.H.TETLEY, ESQ.   GENERAL SECRETARY · FREDERICK J. POTTER

Received with grateful thanks 29th Jan 19

£ 2 : — : —

in aid of Dr Barnardo's Homes

HONORARY TREASURE

The Sheredean Club
Per: Miss Pat Stacey,
66, Sandfield Road,
Arnold, Notts.

N 44593

Head Offices: STEPNEY CAUSEWAY · LONDON · E · I

(England & Wales)

Trevelyan House
St. Stephen's Hill,
St. Albans.

———

Dear Miss. *Stacey + Friends*

Houghton Mill Appeal

Please accept our grateful thanks for

your response to the above appeal.

Official receipt is enclosed.

Yours sincerely,

02786   NATIONAL OFFICE.

22 · 11 · 19 56

Received with many thanks from

Miss Pat Stacey + Friends

DONATION TO
YOUTH HOSTELS ASSOCIATION   £   s.   d.
(ENGLAND AND WALES)   7 · 0

Per *Houghton Mill Fund*

IMPSON,
ccountant.

They even made a donation to the Houghton Mill Appeal

Sheredean Chapter 12

1957

Written by Wendy Stacey, essays, Joyce Parkinson, Mavis Roles, Pat Ellis and Peggy Lowton

I WOULD LIKE TO EXPLAIN first that I (Wendy Stacey) am now continuing the writing of the Log Book, as Pat will be leaving us later this year to get married.

The committee chosen for 1957 was elected as follows, Joyce, Peggy and myself besides Captain (Pat) and Vice Captain (Ann).

At our first meeting we were pleased to welcome Betty Shaw back, and in February a new member Judith Young, came along. Unfortunately she left us in June, however.

Our meetings continued with the usual games and chatter. In March we had a musical evening - with cakes, drinks and 'rock n roll' and in April we started talking about a Youth Hostels Trip to Ilam in May. Here is a report by Joyce.

Ilam Hall Youth Hosteling May 4th and 5th

The Club met in Nottingham, caught a bus to Derby, then from Derby to Ashbourne, we walked to Ilam via Dovedale. Arriving at the Hostel in good time, we signed in, changed our shoes, and made beds.

The Juniors then had to wait till 7-30pm for their supper, while the rest of us self cooked. After a good meal we went outside, and were playing with a ball until it found it's way into the river.

Captain, Vice Captain, Wendy, Peggy and myself decided we would climb 'Bunster Hill'. This we did with much puffing and panting. When we came down, we went to the one and only cafe in Ilam, and had a cold, refreshing, drink.

When we arrived back at the Hostel, we went into the common room, where dancing was in progress. The warden came in at about 11-00pm when we all went to bed.

On Sunday morning we got up at 7-30am after a very sleepless night, due to Pat Ellis's fidgeting. After breakfast, we did our duties, collected our cards, then left the Hostel.

The River Dove being the attraction in that area, we set off along the path at the side of the River. Some of us climbed up to Reynards Cave, where Derek and Graham, who we met at the Hostel, had mashed a cup for us.

From Reynards Cave we walked to Milldale, then on to Alsop-en-le-Dale. At the station we went to the 'Gents' toilet, because the 'Ladies' was locked. After that we found a disused railway truck, where we had our photograph taken.

We then walked down to the New Inn, where we waited for a bus. The car park at the Inn had a notice which stated 'PLEASE PARK PRETTILY'. We gave a demonstration of this , and had a photograph taken doing so.

The girls parking Prettily

On the Derbyshire border

The bus eventually came which took us to Ashbourne. From Ashbourne we caught a bus to Derby, then Derby to Nottingham, after another very enjoyable weekend.

Joyce Parkinson

Later on at one of our evening meetings we cooked our supper and sang camp songs round several small fires up the fields. Everybody seems to enjoy these evenings. Also one evening several of us went swimming at Highfields.

The Seniors decided that they wanted to go hosteling again - this time for a week in the Isle of Wight, but unfortunately only V. Cap, Peggy and Joyce were able to go.

At August Bank Holiday many members of the Club went camping at Annesley Park. Pat Ellis and Mavis Roles will tell you all about it.

Annesley Camp

On Friday the second, of August, Mr Hill came up in the lorry to fetch us all. He arrived just as we had finished getting things ready to be packed, on the lorry. On the way we picked up Joyce, Peggy and Vice Captain. When we got there we had to pitch the tents. I was the one who went underneath but Ann, soon came in so I wasn't so scared, anyway we got them all up. Then we fetched some water. We then thought of having our supper and going to bed, so we made our beds and went straight to bed. Nobody slept very much that night and we were all very tired, in the morning. Peggy Lowton was QM and in the morning she made some breakfast for us, all the Juniors helped her. After dinner we sun bathed and played a bit, then we had our tea, played a bit more and went to bed.

On Sunday morning, we got up and went to Church at 11 o'clock where the Vicar welcomed us. As I was going up for Communion I slipped down the step which made the choir boys laugh, I did feel silly. We had dinner but the steam pudding wasn't done, so we had a slice of cake and custard instead.

Soon after we had had our dinner we sunbathed and did club duties, we also did other things that were useful. We then had tea. Mr and Mrs Hill came and Stevie, who came to see Penny. They stayed until six o'clock. That night we all felt tired so we had an early night. On Monday we were all very busy cooking and collecting wood, fetching water and many other things. So dinner time soon came. Soon after this rest hour came. After rest hour we played on Peggy's trolley and later we had tea. After tea we played on the trolley again. For supper we had biscuits and cocoa. After supper we went to bed.

On Tuesday after breakfast we did our jobs. Then we got ready to go to Annesley Hall. When we were ready it began to rain so we waited till it stopped. Soon we were on the way to the Hall, when we got there we were greeted by Mrs Musters.

She showed us about the house. In one room was a beautiful chandelier. She also showed us some glasses which tinkled when she touched them, also she showed us a music box which started when it was picked up. About half an hour later we were back at camp. We started packing up, Peggy said we were not having any dinner, but of course we did. About six o'clock most of the things were packed. Soon Mr Hill came. About six fifteen we had got all the things on the Lorry. We got home about seven. We took the things back to the shed and then we all went home.

Mavis Roles and Pat Ellis

Soon after this, as Pat was getting very busy with her arrangements for the wedding on September 7th, I began to take club meetings and after the wedding I became Captain.

I must say now that I never realised how difficult it is to arrange meetings and to get something interesting and different going every week. We had several committee meetings to discuss what we were going to do about the club, and in the end it was decided reluctantly that we should give it up at Christmas, as nobody seemed very keen on continuing as Captain. I'm afraid nobody has such good organising powers as Pat.

Then came the great day - at least for Pat and Derek!! - I as bridesmaid was certainly more nervous than Pat, who was doing sewing and eating ham sandwiches immediately before the ceremony. I know all the Club who could, went to the wedding at St Pauls and Joyce will give a few of her impressions.

Captains Wedding 7 Sept 1957

This was a very big event. Captain was married at St Pauls Church, Daybrook, Nottingham by the Revd Keen.

The wedding was at 12-15pm Captain arrived at a very full Church in a beautiful dress of Lace. It was a crinoline skirt, and had a high turn back collar, and long sleeves. The bride was attended by her sister Wendy, and cousin Betty, who both wore pink dresses in net, with white head-dresses. The best man was a friend of Derek Briggs, the Bridegroom.

After the service Captain and Derek walked under two flags formed by a Guard of Honour by the 1st Arnold Guide Company. Many photographs were taken, then the guests were taken up to the Tree Tops Hotel on Mapperley Plains, where the reception was to be held. A good meal was served, and then the speeches were given, which were most inspiring. After the reception Captain and Derek went to change before going away. They left the Tree Tops Hotel to catch the 4-15pm train from Nottingham. They went to Cornwall touring for their honeymoon.

J Parkinson

The Wedding Group

Just after the wedding the membership of the Club seemed to drop off a good deal, and Penny very unfortunately had to stop coming when the dark nights came, as it was too far for her to come - the family having moved to Thackerays Lane. Also Gillian had not been for a long while - she became ill and had to go into a Sanatorium on December 4th. Vice Captain stopped coming after Pat got married, due to her own courting and she became engaged on November 17th, her birthday to another Derrick (spelt differently to Pat's Husband).

However at the beginning of October we had 3 new members come on the same evening - Brenda, Maureen and Rita.

We decided that as we were giving up at Christmas we would go for a last Youth Hosteling trip to Leam Hall near Sheffield, and meet Pat and Derek there, and then go on to see their Bungalow. Peggy, Joyce, Pat and Mavis, Pat Ellis and myself decided to go but a week before I had to drop out as I had an operation on my hands. However they thoroughly enjoyed themselves as shown by these few words from Peggy.

Club Outing to Leam Hall

'Just the right weather for hiking' was one of the last remarks to be said just before we left Nottingham. It really was perfect, but by the time we got into the 'Highlands' of Yorkshire the sky was grey and the air misty.

There were six of us altogether - Pat and Mavis Roles, Pat Ellis, Joyce, Carol (my sister) and myself.

One main attraction of this trip was that we were going on the train - luckily Club were paying the fares. After an uneventful train journey (except for Pat Ellis gorging herself with food) we arrived at 'mucky' Sheffield. From here we caught a bus to Grindleford Bridge and after about a 30 minute walk up what seemed a mountain side we arrived at the Hostel only to join a very long queue of people signing in.

The Hostel was full and the crowd there were a jolly lot despite skirts, high heels and stockings. Perhaps I ought to mention the it was their Xmas Party, but never-the-less we did feel out of it in our sweaters and jeans.

Pat and Derek met us at the Hostel and they with three of the juniors enjoyed a Christmas Dinner which they had had prepared for them. Joyce, Pat E and myself self-cooked, eating in the kitchen because we dare not take our dinner into the dining room where the Xmas dinner was being served.

We spent a very pleasant evening with plenty of party games but we were ready for bed when the time eventually came. As we have experienced so many times before the night was not what it ought to have been. Mavis had to get out of her bunk and woke people up in three dorms, and the other juniors were as usual noisy and fidgety.

At last came a frosty morning and after breakfast we set off on the 'highroad' into Hathersage and then up and up the hills to Burbage Moor. Oh, what a sight, nothing but flat moorland covered with heather which looked white with the frost. The sheep on the moor were quite friendly provided you were willing to feed them. We gave then sweets which they seemed to enjoy very much.

It was up here on the rocks where we had our dinner - some of us wearing our gloves. The wind was really terrible - Brr...! Then after some very tedious but enjoyable rock climbing we started on our way again and the moor was left behind just by crossing a wall and stepping into green fields once more.

It was not long before we would reach Pat's bungalow. There we enjoyed some very welcome food and drink and had a very good look round expressing our admiration and trying to give some useful hints - such as 'Where are the bunks, Pat'?

Derek took us to Sheffield in his car and saw us off on the train. We arrived in Nottingham about 5-45pm from there we made our own ways home after a most enjoyable week-end.

Peggy Lowton

We had another committee meeting after the hosteling trip as Peggy and Joyce had been talking to Pat about the Club carrying on. At this meeting we changed our decision and agreed to take it in turns to take Club meetings, so that I took one two weeks a month and Peggy and Joyce took one each.

Soon we began to have work evenings every week and discussions about the Social to be held in the Conservative Hall on 7 December. A very kind anonymous gentleman offered to pay for the Hall for us when he heard that we worked for Dr Barnardo's Homes.

Thank you very much!

However the Sale and Social was a great success - we had about 70 people there and Pat Roles will tell you a little about it.

Club Social 1957

The Club Social was held at the Conservative Hall, Arnold from 7-30 to 10-00pm, the admission being 1/6.

Most of the club had been there in the afternoon setting out the sale of work and hanging up decorations.

The things on sale did not go very well, which was surprising as there were a pleasing number of people present.

The evening started off with a Barn Dance and was followed by more dancing and games. At 8-30pm refreshments were handed round by the club, consisting of a cob, and cakes, and tea or orangeade.

The refreshments were followed by drawing for the raffle, the tickets of which had been sold during the evening. The raffle prize, a basket of fruit, was won by Mr Briggs.

More dancing and games followed. The evening was finished off by everyone joining in 'Old Lang Syne'.

finished off by everyone ju...

Notice about the social

We made a profit of about £6-15s from the Social, of which £5 was sent to Dr Barnardo's Homes, together with £3 which was collected when we went carol singing. We went two nights this year, and Pat and Derek and my boyfriend Eddie joined us on Christmas Eve. As usual we were invited in at quite a few houses for food and drinks - including our house, Stacey Blakes, Betty's and Pat Ellis's, and we all thoroughly enjoyed ourselves.

Here is the receipt and letter from Dr Barnardo's Homes.

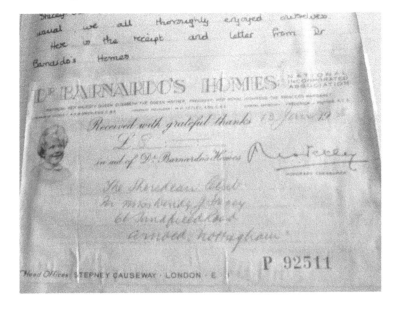

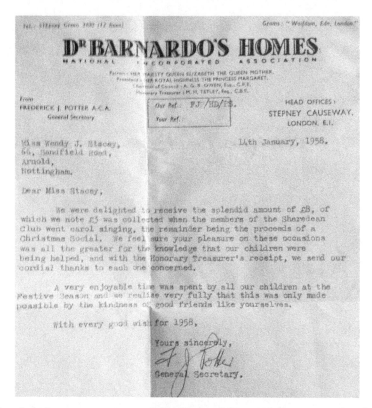

A little while later we sent two dolls, beautifully made by Mavis for the sale and which unfortunately did not sell, to Dr Barnardo's.

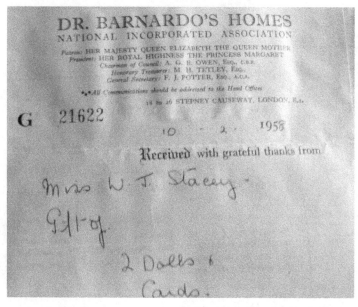

Thank you for the Dolls

Two more pictures sent by Dr Barnardo's

Sheredean Chapter 13

1958
Written by Wendy Stacey, essays, Betty Shaw, Mavis Roles and Pat Ellis

THE NEXT PIECE OF EXCITEMENT that we had was when I got the following letter in the Daily Sketch letter column on February 6th.

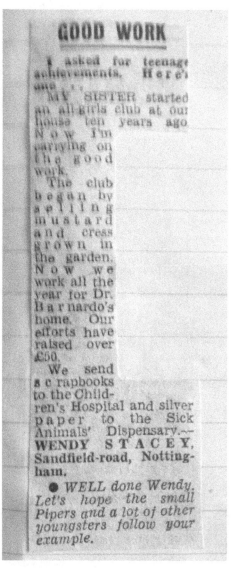

GOOD WORK

I asked for teenage achievements. Here's one :

MY SISTER started an all girls club at our house ten years ago. Now I'm carrying on the good work.

The club began by selling mustard and cress grown in the garden. Now we work all the year for Dr. Barnardo's home. Our efforts have raised over £50.

We send scrapbooks to the Children's Hospital and silver paper to the Sick Animals' Dispensary.— WENDY STACEY, Sandfield-road, Nottingham.

● *WELL done Wendy. Let's hope the small Pipers and a lot of other youngsters follow your example.*

The daily Sketch was a tabloid size daily newspaper which was founded in 1909 and closed on merger with the Daily Mail in 1971

We received quite a few letters from various people and parcels of scraps and silver paper. One lady Mrs Pinnell sent us 10/- as well as a parcel and old cards, and I am continuing writing to her as she seems very interested in the work the club are doing.

Here is the first letter we received from her.

6/2/58

10, Gordon Road,
Surbiton, Surrey

Dear Miss Wendy Tracey,

After reading your letter in the Daily Sketch, I sent some used Christmas & Birthday cards to your address, I considered your letter the Star of the column and was sorry Peter Piper did not think so too, herewith please find a ten shilling note which I hope will ease the disappointment a wee bit, and helps in your good work. It always pleases me when youngsters try to bring happiness to others, more unfortunate than themselves. I am a widowed pensioner, but will keep your address. My best wishes on your club and it's members also the good work you are doing.

Yours faithfully
(Mrs) Ella Pinnell

Cast thy bread upon the waters ye shall find it after many days. This I have proved, and so will you in time.

White Lodge
Blyth Rd
Bromley
Kent

Wednesday

Dear Miss Stacey

Thank you so much for letter
& also all the news of what your club is
doing, & I do hope you will succeed in
all you do, so I am sending on the
carols & do hope you will find them
useful, and also give great pleasure
to the children. How often do you have
a social or Sale of work, the people I am
House keeper to, are very interested in
Dr Barnardo's Homes, as your work is for
a good & cause, & I wish you every
success. & thanking you once again

Yours
sincerely
Miss Hoyblin

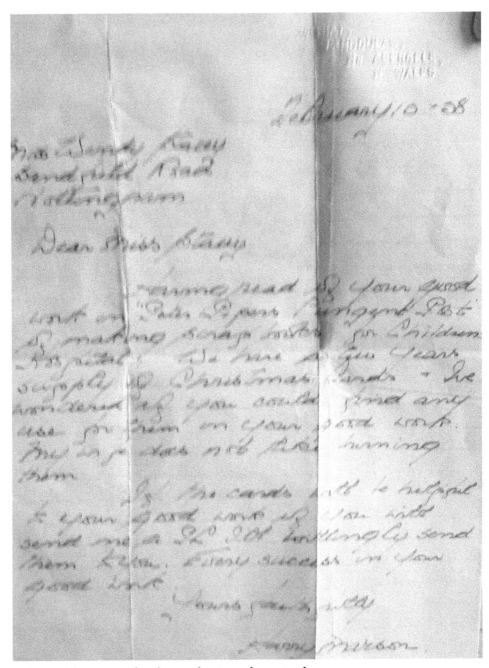

Two of the many other letters that Wendy received

Two new members, Pat Hodson and Susan Jowett joined about this time and were enrolled. Later Cheryl Briggs joined.

Our next excitement was when I took the Club out on a hike one day. Betty will tell you all about it.

It was decided, some weeks earlier, the Club would go on a hike on Good Friday. It was a beautiful day as we all met, and before the hike began we had our photographs taken by Mrs Stacey.

We walked down Rolleston Drive and then along Kiddier Road and straight across Coppice Road, and then turned right up some fields which led on to Mapperley Plains.

Then we walked along the Plains, we turned on to the road leading to Dorket Head and then down the road leading to Calverton.

Before we reached Georges Hill, everyone was thirsty so we sat down on the grass verge and had a drink.

After this refreshment we turned up an old cart track at the top of Georges Hill and this led us by the side of a farm. When we were by this farm we went through some more fields which brought us out at a stream.

We crossed this stream (luckily nobody fell in) and then sat down for some dinner, and had a photograph taken.

We had not been eating for very long when cows appeared at the top corner of the field and started to advance towards us. Wendy, not liking cows very much, quickly gathered up her belongings and fled into the next field, and the rest of us followed.

We managed to get safely away from the animals and then sat down and finished our dinner in peace, and then had a rest.

After this we walked into Woodborough where we all had either an ice scream or a sucker. We walked by Woodborough Church and then up a very steep hill. We went through more fields until we reached Lambley where some of us had another sucker.

To get back onto Mapperley Plains, we decided that the best way would be through the dumbles. We were whistled at by some boys and even followed by one group, but we did not take very much notice of them.

About half way through the Dumbles we had to climb over a fence and then by some mud, well, Carol managed to fall in the mud and when she stood up her jeans were filthy. We all found this episode most amusing.

When we finally reached Mapperley Plains, Eddie (Wendy's boyfriend) was there, and then we all walked down the fields leading back to Rolleston Drive, and from there everyone made their own way home after a most enjoyable hike.

Betty

Before setting out for the Good Friday Hike

Enjoying their 'dinner'

Mr and Mr Stacey, he is just visible in the background

Next we decided to go on a Youth Hostelling trip to Matlock. Here is a report by Mavis.

On Saturday 19th July Wendy, Eddie, Joyce, Tony, Peggy, Pat R, Pat E, Jane, Carol and myself went to Matlock Bath Youth Hostel. We caught the two o'clock bus from Huntingdon Street, Bus Station. We arrived in Matlock Bath about three o'clock. Then we crossed the Derwent and found a hayfield near High Tor. Later, Wendy suggested climbing it. We all went except Joyce and Peggy who stayed behind to look after the rucksacks and to sunbathe. We went in groups and went up different sides of High Tor. We met at the top, where we stopped to have a drink at the restaurant. We eventually found ourselves back in the hayfield where we sat down. Eddie sat on an ant bed. We waited for Tony, Pat E, Jane and Carol came but no Tony. Eventually Wendy found him, Joyce and Peggy had gone into Matlock Bath for a cup of tea and to buy a loaf of bread and a bottle of milk.

At five we started for the hostel without Peggy and Joyce as we couldn't find them. About 5-20 we arrived at the hostel. The two Pats, Jane and Carol slept in dorm 3, Peggy, Wendy, Joyce and myself slept in dorm 1.

Carol, Joyce, Peggy, Pat E, and Tony were self cooking. The hostel supper consisted of tomato soup, potatoes, peas, stuffed ribs and batter; sliced banana, jelly and custard and a cup of tea.

Wendy, Eddie, Joyce and Tony went a walk before and after supper. About 9-30 Peggy asked the remainder if we would like to go to the chip-shop, we went. Joyce was late going to bed and had only just started getting undressed when the warden told us to turn off the lights.

At 7-30 we started getting up. For breakfast which was at 8-30 we had, porridge; bacon, egg, fried bread, tomatoes; bread, butter and marmalade, and a cup of tea.

After we had done our jobs and had three photos taken we moved off as it was about ten. We then walked to Bonsall. When we were walking back to Matlock Eddie managed to push Wendy into a small stream nearby. She tried to push him in but was unsuccessful.

At 12 we stopped near Matlock and had dinner. Then at 2-45 it started to rain so we started to walk to Matlock. We arrived at 3-30. Then we went to a cafe and had a drink. At 6 minutes to 4 we caught the bus, Wendy and Eddie caught the 4 minutes to 6 bus. We arrived in Nottingham about five.

Mavis

A pencil drawing, presumably of Matlock Bath Hostel

On the steps of Matlock Bath Youth Hostel

During August the club did not meet as some of us were on holiday, but we started once more the first week in September.

As the evenings got darker we went inside in the front room, and made our scrapbooks for the Children's Hospital. We also played games etcetera and soon began to talk about the Social which we decided to have on December 6th at the Conservative Hall. This year we thought we would do a sketch and a few little things to entertain. However as no one could find a sketch we could do, I decided to try and write one. This I did and from then on we were rehearsing this (and other things) and making props for it. Also making grass skirts and garlands for our other main item.

A little before this we had decided to have 2 more members on the committee, and Betty and Pat Roles were elected.

We lost three of our new members, Cheryl, Susan and Pat Hodson and Ann Taylor brought a new member, Sandra along, a few weeks before the social.

```
        GRAND SOCIAL EVENING
             to be held by
        THE SHEREDEAN CLUB
                at
    The Conservative Hall, Arnold
                on
      Sat. Dec. 6th at 7 pm.

Admission 1/6 including refreshments
      Proceeds to Dr. Barnados Homes.
```

The typed notice about the social

The Club Social 1958

The Club held a social on December 6th 1958. On Saturday afternoon we went down to practice at the Conservative Hall, Arnold for the evening performance.

First of all, before we could practice, we had to clear away tables and chairs, which had been left by the decorators, but this didn't take long.

We practised the sketch which was called 'In a Psychiatrist's Surgery' also, the Hula, Hula, scene, Songs and other things. We also prepared the 'Sale of Work' ready for the evening.

Slowly but surely the evening came on. People began to turn up, either buying a ticket 1/-6d ticket, or showing us the one they had already bought.

We started the evening with a waltz, then a game. While this was going on Pat and Mavis Roles were selling raffle tickets 3d each. The scene 'In a Psychiatrist's Surgery' came next which was very good. We all thought that Peggy (Lowton) would forget her words, as she didn't know them very well. This was followed by games and dances. Then we had the Hula, Hula, scene. Betty Shaw acted 'The only man on the island', while we others were native girls.

This was followed by refreshments which everybody was ready for. They included tea, squash, cake, sandwiches, cobs and biscuits. Ann Taylor then played 'Forgotten Dreams' on the piano, followed by Ann and myself singing 'Santo Natale'. It was now well into the evening, so we had a game of pass the parcel, one of the forfeits happened to be 'Dance a Tango with Mr Stacey' but he did it very well for a change. Another was to do the Hula Hoop in front of everyone which luckily the girl could do. It was then nearly time to end the evening, so we finished by 'Auld Lang Syne'. The raffle was won by Mrs Dodd who bought us a box of chocolates for another raffle prize, so she deserved the basket of fruit. We then said goodbye to everyone and went home after a very enjoyable evening.

Pat Ellis

As Pat said - we had a lovely evening, and I would like to thank everyone who made it such a successful one. We made approximately £5-10s profit.

Earlier in the year, in October, I had written to Dr Barnardo's asking them for a new collecting box, which they sent together with a credit slip with which they asked us to pay the money into Barclays Bank.

DR. BARNARDO'S HOMES

BARNARDO-DAY FUND

Chairman: BRYAN E. FIGGIS, Esq.
Secretary: ANEURIN JONES, B.A.

AJ/MS

15th October, 1958.

Miss W. J. Stacey,
66, Garfield Road,
Arnold, Nottingham.

Dear Miss Stacey,

Thank you for your letter of the 15th October.
I very much appreciate your kind offer to form a carol party on yet
another occasion, to help maintain our large family of more than
7,500 boys and girls, and I sincerely hope that you and your friends
will have a happy time carolling and that the weather will be kind
to you.

As requested I have been pleased to arrange for
a new collecting box to be sent to you under separate cover. In the
meantime I am enclosing a certificate of authority for collecting
from house-to-house.

In reply to your enquiry regarding the farthings
which you have accumulated. I would suggest that you pay these into
your nearest Branch of Barclays Bank, who will accept them on our
behalf, together with proceeds of your carol singing effort, and I
herewith send you a form for that purpose.

May I take this opportunity of thanking you for
your valued support and I shall look forward to hearing the result of
your effort in due course.

With best wishes

Yours sincerely,

Aneurin Jones

165

The week before Christmas we had our club party to which Mum and Dad were invited. We all brought food and drinks and played games etcetera.

The prizes were given as follows:-

Cup Prize - Mavis

Points Prize - Pat Roles

Attendance Prize - Pat Roles and Mavis

They both did very well. Besides these prizes, we gave Mum a pair of stockings and Dad a box of chocolates. The Club gave me a lovely set of mauve coat hangers and shoe horn.

On Christmas Eve most of the Club met at 7 o'clock to go carol singing. One or two of our boyfriends came with us to make a bit more noise, and later - Pat and Derek joined us. As usual we were invited in at quite a few houses, for food and drinks. This year Betty had made a lantern out of a Swede, and it was very effective. We were able to send £4 this year from our efforts - of which 10/- was from Mrs Dodd, although we had not sung to her. Another 2/- was from a friend of hers, whom had heard of our good work.

Besides this money, we had collected 3/-3d in farthings over a number of years, and I paid this £9-13-3 in to Barclays Bank on the 3rd January 59. Below is the credit slip and over the page the letter and receipt from Dr Barnardo's Homes.

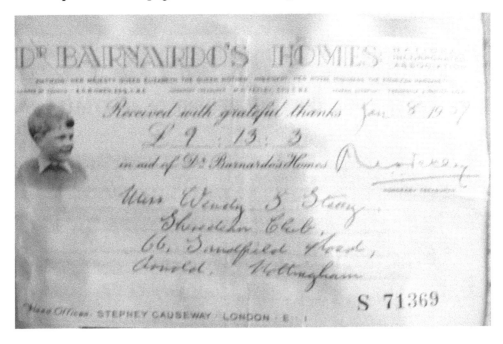

DR. BARNARDO'S HOMES
NATIONAL INCORPORATED ASSOCIATION

Patron:
HER MAJESTY QUEEN ELIZABETH THE QUEEN MOTHER
President: HER ROYAL HIGHNESS THE PRINCESS MARGARET

BARNARDO-DAY FUND

Chairman: BRYAN E. FIGGIS, Esq.
Secretary: ANEURIN JONES, B.A.

Telegrams: JONES, WARDOM, EDO, LONDON
Telephone: STEPNEY GREEN 3400

Head Office: 18-26 STEPNEY CAUSEWAY
LONDON, E.1

AJ/GT

13th January, 1959.

Miss W. I. Stacey,
66, Sandfield Road,
Arnold,
Nottingham.

Dear Miss Stacey,

I have much pleasure in enclosing herewith our Honorary Treasurer's receipt for the welcome sum of £9.13s.3d. being the proceeds of the special efforts arranged by the members of the Sheredean Club at Christmas on behalf of the boys and girls in our care. I shall be glad if you will accept for yourself and convey to all concerned my deep appreciation of this practical help.

We are most grateful to you for coming to our aid so generously, as the task of feeding, clothing and maintaining our large family of more than 7,500 boys and girls is not without its anxiety in these days of constantly rising costs.

I should like to assure you that your gift will assist us greatly in our work and to express the hope that our children may receive the benefit of your help for many years to come.

With renewed warm thanks,

Yours sincerely,

Aneurin Jones

BARCLAYS BANK LIMITED

3 | 1   19 59

Credit the
account of   Dr. Barnardo's Homes,

at   Barnardo Day Fund,   Bank

at Barclays Bank, Bow Branch, Branch
London, E. 3.

				£	s	d
Notes	...	10/-			10	—
„	...	£1	9			
„ over		£1				
Silver	...	...				
Nickel 3d. Pieces	...					
Copper	...	...			3	3
TOTAL CASH	...			9	13	3
Postal Orders	...	...	...			
Cheques, etc. (listed below)			...			

Names of Drawers   Names of Payees

(Carol Account)

Total Credit £   9 | 13 | 3

Paid in by   W. J. Stacey

Sheredean Chapter 14

1959

Written by Wendy Stacey, essay Brenda, Carol, Pat Ellis and Betty Shaw

AT THE BEGINNING OF THE year we had a disappointment because Joyce and Peggy said they were not going to come anymore. However Betty said she would help me take meetings, and the first week she brought a new member Brenda along.

We decided to start the committee afresh this year, so with Betty and I, Pat Roles and Pat Ellis were elected. Various ideas were put forward, such as a musical evening and monopoly, which we did two evenings. Also Ice Skating was suggested, and we decided to try this for the first time. Brenda gives her report.

Ice Skating

On Tuesday the 17th of February we all went ice skating. We met outside Lyons at 7-20. Betty and I were the last to arrive. It was three shillings to get into the Ice Stadium and one shilling to borrow skates. Wendy, Mavis, Pat E, Pat R, and I borrowed skates, Betty's skates did not fit her, so she kindly lent them to Carol. Betty borrowed her skates from a friend. The skates at the Ice Stadium had not got much support at the ankles.

Mavis found it awkward to walk on them so she took one off and hobbled to the rink. Carol said she had not been skating before but proved herself a good skater. Wendy did quite well, Pat Ellis fell down but did not hurt herself. Betty can skate so she helped us all along. At 8-30 Betty and I went downstairs for some refreshment while there was special dancing in progress.

We left the Ice Stadium about nine o'clock and when we arrived in Arnold some of us had some chips. We all said it was a very enjoyable evening.

Brenda

Yes it was, and we must try it again sometime! We decided to go out on Good Friday as usual and Carol will tell you all about it.

Club Hike

On 27th March the club went on a hike to Bleasby. We caught the train from the Midland Station and left at three minutes past ten, which got into Bleasby Station at about 10-30.

It was not pleasant at all in the morning - it even started to rain. On the way we saw a sheep with her two little baby lambs - it looked as if one of the little lambs had only just been born.

When we came to the fields we had to go over them and it was very muddy and Brenda walked through some mud and came out without her shoes, and her feet were covered with mud. Then further down the fields we had dinner. We all had dinner. We had to sit on wet grass. Pat had a tin of tomatoes just on their own, much to our horror!!

Then we walked on over some more fields and came to a dead end - a field leading to gardens, so we had to go down the muddy path which led us to where we were before.

Then we came to St James Church and all of us said how sweet it was. When we came out and closed the gate we all ran down the Road and sat down on a bench. I had my photograph taken lying on a gate, and one of us sitting on a bench eating.

When we were all ready we walked towards the river. When we got there we watched several men boating. As we walked by the river we came to the weir and the Lock and watched the boatmen come through and then we had tea.

After tea we walked down the river to Fiskerton where we caught the train and arrived at the Midland Station at about 6-30pm, and all arrived home at about 7-20pm after a wonderful day.

Carol

Here are some photos which we took.

We had the usual club meetings after this - outside when the light nights came and had an evening cooking our supper on the fields. We had about half a dozen small boys watching us most of the time, and of course we all roared with laughter when Betty's frying pan caught fire!

We decided to have 2 months holiday in July and August, but decided to go to Skegness for a day in July. Pat's report follows.

Skegness Outing

On Saturday 26th of July the club spent a day at Skegness. We caught the bus down to Victoria Station at about 8-00am, at the Station we met Dorothy, one of Betty's friends, and Eddie. We then caught the 9-25am train to Skegness arriving there at 11-30am.

At 12 o'clock we met Pat and Derek Briggs, and after that we made our way onto the beach where we stayed most of the day. With the weather being very warm, we all had a good swim despite the jelly-fish which were floating around.

Fun started when we were getting changed, I think Pat (Briggs) was the only one who managed to get dressed easily. The rest of us just howled with laughter all the time, especially at the two boys - we took some smashing photos of them.

After having tea we made our way to the fun fair. Most of us went on the Big

Wheel, some on the Rocket and on the Waltzers and Big Dipper.

Then we made our way to the Boating Lake. Dorothy and I had a boat. It's a wonder we didn't drown, if some boys hadn't been so helpful I'm sure we would have done.

At last it was time to go home. We said goodbye to Pat and Derek as they were catching a different train and then we caught the next train and we arrived home after spending a wonderful day.

Patricia Ellis

Betty and Eddie on the big wheel

Mavis, Pat E., Pat R.

We started meeting again in September and Carol brought along a new member, Deidre, who had been for a few weeks in 1958. We soon started meeting inside, and discussions and work for the sale of work for the Social and Sale of Work were started.

(A magazine cutting is inserted in the Sheredean log book with no explanation but it indicates why Pat, Wendy and the girls were dedicated to sending funds to Dr Barnardo's Homes. I have included the story into the text of this book because readers may not be able to read it clearly from the pictures that I also include, MP.)

The Story of Dr Barnardo

Tom Barnardo came to London from Dublin at the age of 21. He was training at the London Hospital in Whitechapel to be a medical missionary in China.

Only four years before Tom Paine had been his favourite author; Paine thought Christianity 'little and ridiculous.' But Barnardo's mother and two brothers became enthusiastic Christians. As they prayed and talked to him his cynicism left him until finally he could say: "I felt that Jesus had indeed died for me."

In London he soon had his own 'ragged school' in a disused stable. There he had a crowd of dirty, illiterate, noisy children.

One night, as he was shutting up, a boy of ten with a 'small stunted frame ... without either shirt, shoes or stockings' pleaded to be allowed to stay.

"Come on, your mother will wonder what keeps you out so late." "I ain't got no mother ... ain't got no father ... ain't got no friends. Don't live nowhere."

Jim Jarvis found a home that night and this was the beginning: Barnardo soon had 25 living in his house in Stepney. Bit by bit, he saw that this was his life's work.

At a missionary meeting he was asked to say a few words about his work. Afterwards a servant girl came up to him and handed him an envelope: "Let me give this, which I had brought for the heathen, to your poor children."

It was 27 farthings. It was the first public money he had received.

Barnardo's work began to grow. Then one day in 1871, he had five vacancies to fill: there were 73 destitute boys to choose from. One ugly 11 year old, with matted red hair pleaded so hard that Dr Barnardo promised to take him in a week's time.

A few days later Barnardo read in the paper of 'Carrots death from exposure and want of food.'

This death moved him to an astonishing act of faith. He hung a sign-board outside his house: 'No destitute child ever refused admission.' He had no certainty of funds; yet never lacked them.

A poor girls farthings, a poor boys death, and a family's love for Jesus have grown into a work which thousands bless.

The story of Dr. Barnardo

TOM BARNARDO came to London from Dublin at the age of 21. He was training at the London Hospital in Whitechapel to be a medical missionary in China.

Only four years before Tom Paine had been his favourite author: Paine thought Christianity 'little and ridiculous.' But Barnardo's mother and two brothers became enthusiastic Christians. As they prayed and talked to him his cynicism left him until finally he could say: "I felt that Jesus had indeed died for me."

In London he soon had his own 'ragged school' in a disused stable. There he had a crowd of dirty, illiterate, noisy children.

One night, as he was shutting up, a boy of ten with a 'small, spare, stunted frame . . . without either shirt, shoes or stockings' pleaded to be allowed to stay.

"Come on, your mother will wonder what keeps you so late."

"I ain't got no mother . . . ain't got no father . . . ain't got no friends. Don't live nowhere."

Top part of the Barnardo story

JIM JARVIS found a home that night and this was the beginning: Barnardo soon had 25 living in his house in Stepney. Bit by bit he saw this was his life's work.

At a missionary meeting, he was asked to say a few words about his work. Afterwards a servant girl came up to him and handed him an envelope: "Let me give this, which I had brought for the heathen, to your poor children."

It was 27 farthings. It was the first public money he had received.

BARNARDO'S work began to grow. Then, one day in 1871, he had five vacancies to fill: there were 73 destitute boys to choose from. One ugly 11-year-old, with matted red hair pleaded so hard that Dr. Barnardo promised to take him in a week's time.

A few days later Barnardo read in the paper of 'Carrot's' death from exposure and want of food.

This death moved him to an astonishing act of faith. He hung a sign-board outside his house: 'No destitute child ever refused admission.' He had no certainty of funds; yet never lacked them.

A poor girl's farthings, a poor boy's death, and a family's love for Jesus have grown into a work which thousands bless.

Lower part of Barnardo story

Towards the end of September Pat Ellis brought along two new members, Sandra Wood and Christine Nelson.

We arranged to have the social on December 12th and we were very busy every Tuesday evening, sewing, doing embroidery and making Christmas logs and snowmen for the sale. We also sent a parcel of silver paper to Tinker Bell at the Nottingham Evening Post.

Sandra and Christine also brought along a new member, Teresa Andrews, a few weeks before the social. Now Betty will tell you all about the evening.

Club Social 1959

On Saturday, December 12th 1959 we held our annual Club Social at the Conservative Hall, Arnold.

The social commenced at 6-45pm with a sale of work, with Christine and Sandra in charge. I was on the door, Teresa was on the bottle stall and the others were selling raffle tickets, for which the prizes were two baskets of fruit and groceries.

We commenced with a few games for the younger ones, and then we had some dancing. At about 8-30 we started getting refreshments ready which were a glass of orange cordial or a cup of tea, and some cakes and biscuits. Immediately after refreshments the Club lined up, complete with lanterns made from turnips, for a session of carol singing, which the audience helped us along with, afterwards we had more dances and games. The social continued until about 10-15pm, when the fog came down and people started to get away before it got too thick.

After everyone had gone, some of the Clubs old members helped us to wash the pots and tidy up the hall, after a most enjoyable evening.

Betty Shaw

This was the notice for the social

When I counted up the money afterwards, I was most surprised and pleased to see that we had made a profit of over £14. Well-done everyone! They all worked very hard, I must say.

Our next excitement was the Club Party - held on the Tuesday evening before Christmas, to which Mum and Dad were invited.

The prizes were given as follows:-

Cup prize - Pat Ellis

Points prize - Mavis

Attendance prizes -

Betty - with 40 out of 40

Mavis - with 39 out of 40

We also gave Mum some soap and bath salts, and Dad some handkerchiefs, and the Club gave me a pair of stockings.

We had decided to go Carol Singing twice this year, but only 5 of us went the first night although 2 of my friends very kindly helped us out. On Christmas Eve Pat and Derek joined us, and we went to Mrs Dolby's and were invited into her cottage to sing. She had been collecting for us and it gave us a good start to the evening. We were also invited in at Mrs Dodds and Mrs Briggs, our house and Stacey Blakes.

With the proceeds from this and the social we were able to send £18 in all to Dr Barnardo's Homes, which was nearly twice as much as last year.

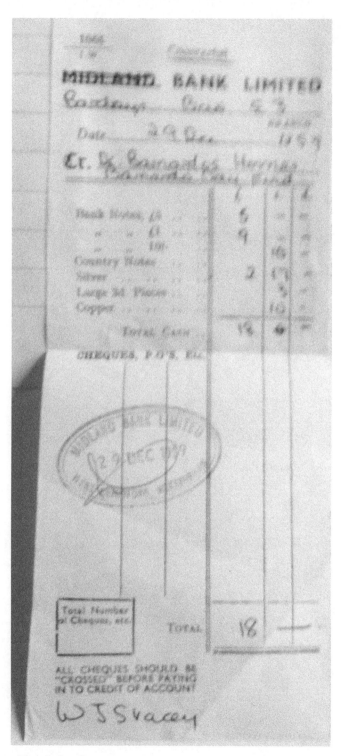

Notice the old style bank receipt

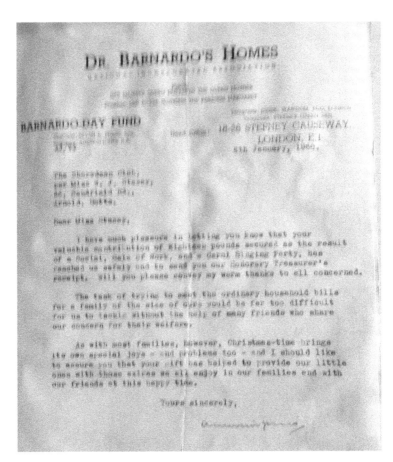

The usual thank you letter

The receipt

Sheredean Chapter 15

1960
Written by Wendy Stacey, essays Teresa Andrews and Mavis Roles

ON THE FIRST CLUB EVENING of the New Year, new member Teresa brought along her sister Jennifer. I had bought some scrapbooks so we set on with doing them. On the third week another member, Janet came brought by Mavis, and we had a table tennis evening.

We also decided that we would have our annual social and sale, so I bought some embroidery etcetera to get on with.

A lot later on we wanted to go for a hike on Good Friday and we worked out that the bluebells would be out, and so decided to go to Epperstone Woods this year. (I believe that it is known as Ploughman Wood in 2019 MP.)

Teresa will tell you all about it.

The Good-Friday Hike

On Good Friday myself, Christine, Wendy, Pat and Mavis set out for a hike to Epperstone Woods. We met at the corner of Coppice Road at 10 o'clock and set off across the corn fields to Mapperley Plains. As we were walking down into Woodborough, Wendy found half a crown. Then when we reached the nearest ice cream shop she bought us all an ice cream.

We arrived at Epperstone Woods about 12 o'clock, had our lunch and then picked some blue-bells, primroses and wood anemones. Then we neared the end of the wood and began to pick flowers very fast. We then crossed some fields and when we were in Epperstone we sat down on a seat and had something else to eat. Now we had two hours in which to look round Epperstone; we walked along and up a small hill. Facing us was a steep hill and Christine and I did not fancy walking up the hill so we waited at the bottom. After about 15 minutes the others appeared and we went back to the Cross Keys and caught the bus home.

Teresa Andrews

Teresa did not mention that they met a goat

I might add that we all came home for half fare!!! As the summer came on we moved down the garden; and also went up the fields, cooking our supper. We had two evenings at Carrington Lido, and although the weather wasn't exactly boiling hot those that went enjoyed themselves thoroughly.

Before we broke up for our 'summer holiday' we decided another outing to Skegness would be exciting. Mavis will write about it.

Skegness Outing 1960

Wendy, Betty, Brenda, Janet, Pat R, and myself met at the end of Sandfield Road at 9.10 on Sunday the 24th of July. We walked down the hill and caught the 52 bus outside the library. Pat E and her boyfriend caught the bus at the 'Conservative Hall.' At Victoria Station we met Eddie and his friend Garth who was going on an outing with the St Martins youth club.

We caught the 9-25 train and arrived at Skegness at 11-30 o'clock. From the station we walked down to the beach and found a sand dune to sit by. Wendy, Betty, Janet, Pat R, Eddie and Garth went down to the sea to paddle and they got thoroughly 'muddied up.' When they came back we ate our sandwiches and then sunbathed. Pat and Janet changed into their bathing costumes and went swimming. Pat E, Malcolm, Betty, Brenda and Garth left us to go round the fun fair and to find a place to have tea.

It then started to rain slightly but not a lot, Pat and Janet came out of the water and changed, they then played with a beach ball for about three quarters of an hour. About 3-45, the remainder of us set off to look round the fun fair. When we arrived there Eddie and Wendy left us. We (Pat R, Janet and myself) left the funfair and walked round the boating lake: we sat by the lake and ate our tea.

By this time it was raining heavily, but was soon over. When we reached the station it started raining again, so we sat down and waited for the others. As it was nearing 8 o'clock we decided to go on the train and find a compartment. We saw Wendy and Eddie who said we could go in their compartment. After some fuss with the youth club we moved down the train and found another compartment.

The train arrived Victoria Station about 10-45pm and most of us arrived home by 11-15.

Mavis Roles

In the dunes at Skegness

When we started meetings again in September our main item on the agenda was the Social. This was to be held on December 3rd at the usual place, so we all got on with something towards the sale.

We had a very successful evening as usual and made a profit of £13-10/. We decided to combine our usual Christmas party with the Social and gave out the prizes during the evening.

Prizes as follows:-

Attendance - Mavis - 31/34

Points - Mavis -120 points

Cup - Teresa - 6 times

We also gave Mr and Mrs Stacey a gift of two towels.

```
THE   SHEREDEAN   CLUB

      invite you to a

GRAND  CHRISTMAS  SOCIAL
        in   aid   of
DR.  BARNARDOS  HOMES
            at
The Conservative Hall, Arnold.
      SAT.  DEC.  3rd
Commencing with a Sale of Work at 7 p.m

  Admission 1/6 including refreshments,
```

The notice about the Social

On Christmas Eve we met for our carol-singing party, and I am very pleased to say that several old members and friends of the club joined us, and at one time we were more than 20 strong! After doing the usual rounds, which were met with the usual generous contributions, the older members went down to the Friar Tuck to ask permission to sing in the bar. Fortunately the publican was very interested in the work for Dr Barnardo's, and we spent about an hour singing and collecting money.

When we got home we were very gratified to learn that we had collected nearly £4-10s - the most I think we have ever collected in a nights singing.

Here is the receipt and letter received from Dr Barnardo's, for the whole amount of £18 (the same as last year).

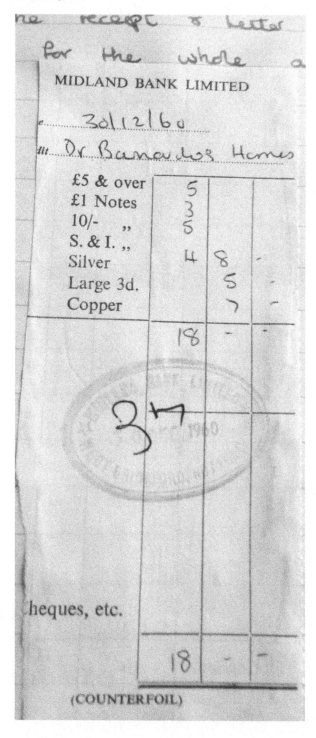

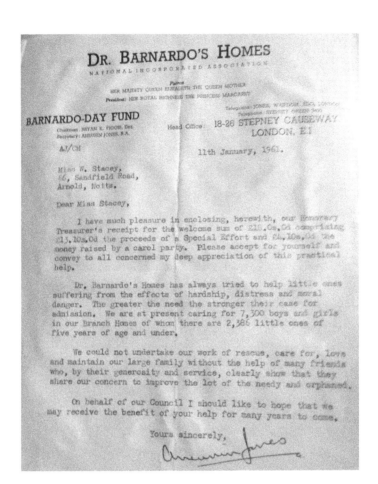

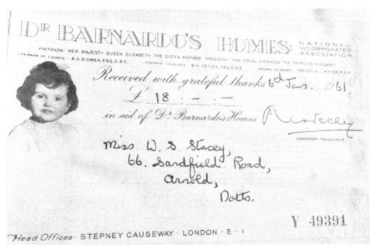

(This was the final year of the Sheredean Club but the Log Books contained further information about the total donations to Dr Barnardo's, reunions and letters which I will record in chapter 16 - MP.)

Sheredean Chapter 16

Written by Michael Parkinson
Final donations and reunions 1961 to 2016

THE PREVIOUS CHAPTER DESCRIBED THE final year of the Sheredean Club but the story did not end there because the second log book contained more information and pictures. There is a list of the money donated to Dr Barnardo's over the years

Amounts sent to Dr Barnardo's over the years

	£	s	d
1947	-	13	6
1948	2	12	-
1949	1	19	3½
1950	-	7	2½
1951	4	18	6
1952	3	6	11
1953	2	-	-
1954	10	15	-
1955	4	7	-
1956	5	-	-
1957	2	-	-
1958	8	-	-
1959	9	13	3
1960	18	-	-
1961	18	-	-
Total	**91**	**12**	**8**

Wendy wrote, 'Rosemary gave me the 7/-4d to make it up to a round figure of £92 and the receipt is overleaf. Let's hope we can make it £100 before too long'.

I estimate that the money donated between 1947 and 1961 equates to over £2200 as I write in 2019.

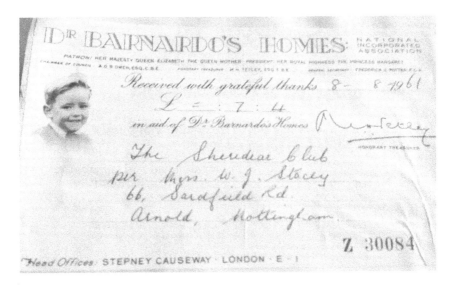

The receipt

Back in 1956, when Pat was planning to get married she handed over the running of the Club to her sister Wendy and planned that girls who had been members of the Club should meet at intervals of 10 years. In preparation for this she encouraged girls to sign a declaration that they would meet at the entrance to Nottingham Castle on the first Saturday of June 1961, 2-30pm and again in 1971.

The first reunion on 3 June 1961 was attended by 11 adults and one baby.

Picture of the 1961 reunion

The second reunion took place on 5 June 1971, again at Nottingham Castle. Wendy wrote in the log book 'I managed to get in touch with about 15 of the 24 members who had signed the log book saying they hoped to come to our twenty year reunion'.

She received many replies and 9 were able to attend with 6 husbands and 12 children. All the letters are placed in the log book and Wendy described the reunion:-

Of those I expected to turn up on June 5th, only one, Joy, didn't, but 2 unexpected members, Pat Stanton (Ellis) and Betty Poole (Shaw) came instead so there were 9 old members present plus 6 husbands and 12 children.

It was, weatherwise, a great contrast to our 10 year reunion, when we had a lovely sunny day. June 5th 1971, was cold and dismal although not raining, fortunately, so we were able to have a picnic and a good chat in the Castle grounds.

The husbands who came proved very useful for looking after the children and running round buying sandwiches etcetera! Thank you!

At about 5-30pm, Rosemary, Ann and Derrick, José and family and Joyce and family decided they would make an evening of it and come back to Whissendine with Pat and I (Pat and co staying with us, up from Somerset). Unfortunately José and family had to drop out at West Bridgford as they were having trouble with the car, which made them an hour and a quarter late for the reunion. The rest of us enjoyed a good old natter and endless cups of tea and food (it seemed) at Whissendine until about midnight, when they all departed.

During the afternoon at the Castle, it was agreed to meet again in another ten years time, first Saturday in June, 1981, 2-30 same place, so I wonder who will turn up then and if we will be recognised? We all seemed to recognise each other this time except I thought Pat (Ellis) was Meresia!

It was also agreed to spend the Club money (about £9) on sending any good photos taken during the afternoon, round to all members who came to the reunion or who had written to me. The rest of the money to go back into the bank for at least another ten years.

Wendy Stevensen (Stacey)

The reunion on 6 June 1981 was attended by 11 old members with (one travelling from Ontario in Canada with two children) plus 21 relatives and children. Pat wrote the report in the log book:-

I came up from Somerset to Hickling for the weekend with Derek and Peter (Michael stayed at home). Wendy asked us to go into Nottingham early as we had to meet Rosemary (Neal) from Canada off the train, she was in London visiting relations. She arrived on time and we escorted her to a cafe, so that we were out of the rain and so that she could find somewhere to eat.

By 2-30 the rain had stopped, and it managed to stay fine for the rest of the day but it was very windy. As we arrived a group of 'old girls' were already chatting and sorting out who was who. Within the next half hour the others had arrived, making 11 of us in all, plus 4 husbands and 5 children. After sitting on the wall outside the Castle for some time, we decided to go inside the grounds and we found a cafe, ordered drinks and chatted some more, we passed around lots of photos, the log books and photo albums.

The afternoon passed very quickly, and soon some members had to depart to make their way home. Others managed to get into Eddies and Dereks cars, and we went out to Hickling, where Wendy and Mum had arranged a buffet tea. Mum and Pop were pleased to meet some of the 'old girls' and she made us all very welcome. More chatting!! Back to Nottingham for 8pm to see Rosemary (Neal) back onto the train. Joyce was collected by her husband and José and Alan went to look for a train or a bus. We then drove to Sherwood, took Joy home and on to Arnold to take Rosemary, we all went in to see Mr Lockley and to ask after Mrs Lockley who is in Hospital. A very happy and interesting day, to be repeated again in 1991. Two photos were sent to each member afterwards, paid for out of Club funds.

Pat Briggs (Stacey)

They signed a pledge to meet at the castle

ON JUNE 6 Nottingham Castle will once again be the meeting place for the ten-yearly reunion of former members of the Sheredean Club, including one from Canada.

The club was started in 1945 at Arnold by Mrs. Pat Briggs, (nee Stacey), who now lives in Somerset.

Meetings took place at her home in Sandfield Road, and when she married it was continued by her sister, Mrs. Wendy Stevenson, now living in Whissendine near Melton Mowbray.

The members did a lot of fund-raising work for Dr. Barnardo's, such as carol singing and concerts.

Disbanded

When the club disbanded in 1960, a book of its history was compiled which contained reports, photographs and press cuttings of their activities including hikes, camping trips and visits to the seaside.

All members signed the book as a pledge that they would attend a reunion at the Castle on the first Saturday in June every ten years.

The first was held in 1961, and the second one in 1971 was attended by nine former members, six of their husbands and 12 children.

Mrs. Stevenson estimates there must be about 30 former members altogether, but some have lost touch. Although some have moved away — including one who lives in Australia — most are believed to have remained in the Nottingham area.

She would like to hear from them and can be contacted at 11 Main Street, Whissendine, Oakham, Rutland or on Whissendine 691.

The cutting from the Nottingham Evening Post

194

Rosemary, Joy, Pat, Penny, Rosemary, Pat, Betty
Joyce, Wendy, Ann, Jose.

Eleven old members at Nottingham Castle

The next reunion was at Nottingham Castle on 1 June 1991, Pat wrote:-

Derek and I arrived with Wendy just before 2-30, and were pleased to meet Rosemary (Lockley), Ann and Brian, Betty, John and son Michael, Penny Starbuck, all but one had their club badges on!

We had a few photos taken outside the castle, then headed for the cafe, so we could sit where it was a little warmer. We had two cups of tea each, looked at the log books and Captains photo albums, which showed some Club activities, plus pictures of Michael and Peter's weddings.

Eighteen months ago my father re-married, and when he heard about the Club reunion he sent his best wishes to all the members. We hunted through the log books to see what year we invested in our smart metal badges, and discovered it was 1954.

In 1986 we sent the final amount of money (£9-00) to Dr Barnardo's, so that we could close the account. At about 4pm we walked to the band stand area of the Castle grounds and sat for a short while in the sun - more photo's and chat. It was rather cold, and some members had to make tracks for home.

Penny was the only one who was able to take up Wendy's offer of tea at Whissendine (near Melton Mowbray, where she and Eddie lived) and after much discussion of how she should find her way, it was suggested that Wendy could go with her to direct her there, while Derek took me back - much laughter that we hadn't thought of that earlier!!

All members wished to meet again in another ten years - and so it was decided to do that, we noted that wheel chairs are available to use in the Castle grounds!!!

Pat Briggs

RSS/EAN

Received with grateful thanks

£ 9 :—

in aid of Dr Barnardo's

MRS. P. A. BRIGGS
PORTHMOOR
36 OLD RD
NORTH PETHERTON
BRIDGWATER
SOMERSET

30th May 1986

Mrs P A Briggs
Porthmoor
36 Old Road
North Petherton
Bridgwater
Somerset
TA6 6TG

Dear Mrs Briggs,

Thank you so much for your donation of £9.00 for which I
our official receipt, and for the copies of informatio
your log book. It was most interesting to read of your
activities all those years ago.

Although our work has changed we still rely on peop
yourself to enable us to continue caring for our childre
of whom are handicapped, either physically, mentally or s
Last year we helped 14,000 boys and girls.

With renewed thanks and best wishes.

Yours sincerely,

R. S. Show
Regional Appeals Director
Wales and the West

The final donation to Dr Barnardo's

Another reunion took place in the Rose Gardens at Arnold Park on 2 June 2001 (close to the house where I spent my childhood days). It was attended by Pat and Derek, Wendy and Eddie, Joyce, Rosemary Lockley, Betty Poole (Shaw), Ann, José and many of their partners and family. Later on they went along to a Supermarket in Arnold for refreshments, they decided that the next get together should be in five years time, making it 2006.

Alan, Wendy, Pat, Eddie, John, Betty, Joyce, Rosemary, Derek, Ann

Arnold Park was again the venue for the reunion on 3 June 2006. Those attending were Pat and Derek Briggs, Wendy and Eddie Stevenson, Betty, José, Rosemary, Ann and Joyce, with partners and many family members.

Picture taken on 3 June 2006

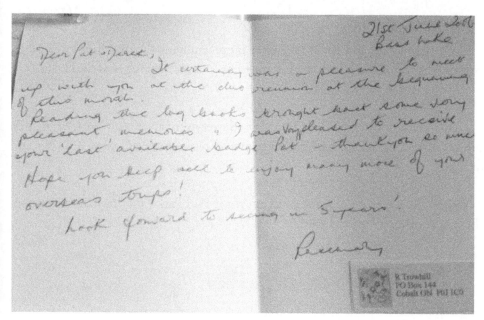

From Rosemary Trowhill (nee Neal) Ontario, Canada

Another reunion of the Sheredean Club took place on 4 June 2011. Pat asked people who attended to write notes in the log book which I include here:-

Reunion at Arnold Park 4 June 2011

José here, starting off the page.

How lovely for us to meet again, all looking well and happy. Going through the club books shows how much we had done when the club was active. Would be nice to keep the information somehow, nothing like our club now days as future children would be amazed. My own grandchildren certainly are.

José

Betty, second to comment.

Just been looking through the books. Lovely to see the photos again. Everyone looking fine and so nice to meet up again. My own children would die if they saw themselves in here.

Betty

Margaret R added her comments.

We are here again to meet each other and enjoy our memories of good times we have had together. It's a day of fine weather we enjoyed after a hard winter. This is the last meal but it doesn't mean we shall not remember each other afterwards. Love to all always.

Margaret xx

Hello again, Ann and Brian here once more, enjoying the fine afternoon. Not a great deal has happened since the last meeting, at least nothing to write about.

Ann

Here's Joyce. How time flies! Recognised everyone but not all 'partner' names. Family all well, grandchildren growing up and moving on, enjoying holidays and gardening.

Joyce

Wendy - lovely to have seven of us at Arnot Hill Park - may have a meal somewhere in another five years!

Wendy

Pat wrote this final entry in the log book:-

Arnold History Group contacted 15-8-11. The group would keep the log books for us based at Arnold Library.

Pat Briggs

Although there is no mention of it in the log book, I have been informed that a final reunion took place at Arnot Hill Park, Arnold, Nottingham on 4 June 2016. It was attended by Pat Briggs, their son Peter and his wife, Jacqui with children Ronan and Cerys. José and husband Alan, Betty Poole (nee Shaw) and her husband, John, Ann Morgan (nee Parkinson), and Margaret Riley (nee Whitt). Pat had arranged that the Chairman of the Arnold Local History Group, Peter Hunt, would meet the group in the Rose Garden and Pat handed the Sheredean Log Books to him. Pat was under the impression that the books would be stored in the Arnold Library but in fact they were stored in the archives of the Arnold Local History Group. Ann remembers that it was a lovely sunny day for that final reunion and that most of the group went to the Old Spot public House on Mansfield Road, Daybrook where they enjoyed their final meal together.

At the 'Old Spot' on 4 June 2016

That was indeed the final reunion of the Sheredean Club. It has been a fascinating experience compiling this book because as the brother of Ann and Joyce I am proud of the contribution that both of them played in helping Pat and Wendy run the club as they were members for most of the years that the club existed. Indeed, working on this project has been like reliving my childhood, going back to listening to the Ovaltineys on Radio Luxembourg, and being brought up to believe that putting concerts on was just a normal thing to do.

I have relied heavily on obtaining information from Mrs Pat Briggs by telephone and letters to check and explain many things that I did not understand and decided that It would be good to meet her in person to complete the procedure and obtain photographs and documents. This proved to be a remarkable story in itself:-

Meeting, Pat Briggs and Michael Parkinson 5 December 2018

Pat Stacey, the 12 year old girl who founded Sheredean Club in 1945 is now 85 Mrs Pat Briggs who lives at North Petherton, near Bridgwater in Somerset. In September 2018 I suggested to my sister Mrs Ann Morgan and my wife Joan that we could go to Western-super-Mare for a few days from Monday 3 December to Friday 7 December 2018 and go to meet Pat on Wednesday 5 December for discussions about this book. We agreed that it would be a good idea and made plans to stay at the Royal Hotel, on South Parade at Weston. We decided to travel by train and booked return tickets.

On Monday 3 December we started the outward journey from East Midlands Parkway station at 10-53am and were scheduled to arrive at Weston-super-Mare at 2-25pm with changes at Derby, and Bristol Temple Meads. We were looking forward to the journey, sitting together, and enjoying the view from the window. We had a whole carriage to ourselves on the first leg of the journey from East Midlands Parkway to Derby. That is where the enjoyment ended because at Derby we discovered that our train to Bristol had been cancelled due to a broken down train. We eventually had to board an over crowded train that was bound for Reading and had to get off at Birmingham New Street, we were not able to sit together, in fact, we were only able to sit because we were old and people gave their seats up for us. At Birmingham, New Street Station we suffered a long delay before we were told to board a train bound for Bristol Temple Meads, this was again vastly over crowded but it was at least going to Bristol, so we were told, but as the train approached Gloucester an announcement was made that the train would terminate there and everyone would have to get off but with no explanation of what we should do. All the passengers had to jostle for a standing position on the platform with no knowledge of what we should do. After about ten minutes an announcement was made that we should transfer to another platform and board a train bound for Cardiff. Again this train was badly overcrowded and we discovered that it was travelling on the opposite side of the Seven Estuary to Bristol but another announcement told us to get off the train at Newport where we had to get on another overcrowded train to Bristol Temple Meads. At Bristol we got on a train which took us to Weston-super-Mare where we arrived nearly three hours late. We booked into the Royal Hotel, went out for a meal and on return to the Hotel enjoyed a glass of wine in the Feathers Bar.

After breakfast on Tuesday 4 December we enjoyed a stroll on the New Grand Pier before I was given permission to walk along the coast on my own as the ladies wanted to look round the shops so we planned to meet back at the Hotel late in the afternoon. Readers can see my video on YouTube with the title *Western-super-Mare to Keystoke, Coast walk with Michael Parkinson,* Ann and Joan can be seen at the start of the video. I was enjoying my walk until Joan phoned in mid afternoon and told me that Ann had been knocked over by a man who was running, out of control in the shopping mall. Someone said that the man had shouted 'get out of my way' before colliding with Ann and knocking her to the ground. She was bruised, bleeding, and shocked but the staff of 'Boots the Chemists' attended to her and said that she did not need to go to hospital. The man said he was sorry before rushing off. That, of course was the end of them enjoying looking round the shops. Joan took Ann back to the Royal Hotel where she rested for a few hours before deciding that she would join Joan and I for a glass of wine in the evening.

Wednesday 5th December was the day that we had arranged to travel to North Petherton to meet Pat Briggs, Ann told us at breakfast that she would still go although she was not feeling great. I said 'after our experiences of Monday and Tuesday at least we had only got to get a taxi from the hotel to Weston and two stops on the train to Bridgwater and then a taxi to Pat's place so at least nothing would go wrong that day'. I was wrong, we got a taxi to the station at Weston and were dropped in plenty of time for our train but on entering the station we were told that there was a 'jumper' on the bridge and all trains were cancelled'. I went back out to the taxi rank and negotiated a deal with a driver who agreed to take us to Pat's address. As the taxi went along the bridge over Weston station we saw the man who had climbed over the railings and was being spoken to by police. We found out later that the man was eventually dissuaded from jumping but it was three hours before the road and rail traffic could move again. Because of the taxi taking us directly to Pat's bungalow we arrived early and conducted our business with Pat who had arranged to take us to her local cafe at lunch time. The place was called 'Tea Birds' at 97 Front Street, North Petherton and they were doing a Christmas Dinner which was lovely and the staff made us very welcome. I wanted to make sure that I got the names right of the people at Tea Birds and so I sent a message, this is the reply,

Hello Michael,

I hope you are well. I remember you visiting well. My name is Sherie-Anne Perry and my daughters name is Leah Geen. Leah turned 8 a few days after your visit and is still very much in charge of all the important jobs.

Best wishes Sherie-Anne.

We went back to Pat's place after lunch and in mid afternoon we checked that the trains were running again before getting a taxi to Bridgwater Station for our journey back to Weston. When the train arrived we had to pull ourselves up a very high step from the platform to the train and were offered no help by the railway staff. We arrived safely back at the Royal Hotel and enjoyed a glass of wine in the evening. Thursday 6 December was a trouble free day and we returned home on Friday but again the train from Bristol to Derby was grossly overcrowded. I completed a claim form for the outward journey delay and six weeks later received full refund from Cross Country Trains for the outward and return journeys with an explanation that a train had hit a deer near Bristol causing damage to the engine.

Whilst concluding writing this book I asked a few of the surviving members to give their general memories of the Sheredean Club and include a few comments. Although the surnames have changed I have used their childhood names so that readers can identify them as writers of some essays included in the logbooks.

José Packwood

Mr Stacey was brilliant he organised 'Holidays at Home' a week full of activities, things for children in the daytime and dances for the grown ups, all on the lawns in front of the council offices in Arnold Park. He got all sorts of folk involved, bands to play, and I can still 'see' folk jitterbugging on those lawns (some in uniform). There were trips around the lake (goodness knows where he got the boats and the folk to handle them). You could pay to have a horse ride, (led if you didn't ride) along one of the quiet back paths in the park. The whole thing was really very good. I met my first boyfriend doing that! For a whole week there was 'entertainment' his idea was because of the way folk weren't having holidays after the war, why not have a week of, Holidays at Home? He was an excellent Master of Ceremonies. All this is of course is nothing to do with the Sheredeaners but just thought it would amuse you as in our little shows he came along and gave us constructive criticism and help. The senior Stacey's were great but very careful to let it all be 'our thing' so that it all worked or not, by us. They must have felt that their garden wasn't their own at times! Anyway sorry to ramble on, good luck with your book, look forward to seeing it.

Very Best Wishes, José

Ann Parkinson

Remembering the years spent with the Sheredean Club, one memory that stands out the most is how welcome we all were at Pat's House. Mrs Stacey was usually there and was always busy and happy to talk about the garden and how she used to mow the immaculate large lawn at the back of the house every day when possible using a push mower without the grass box so that there never any clipping which needed to be picked up. I spent a lot of time there. During the winter months our club meetings were in the house playing board games. One of the most popular was called beetle and we all had great fun drawing strange beetles.

Betty Shaw

Dear Michael, Thank you so much for your letter re the Sheredean Club and the fact that you are writing a book about it. How lovely to think that it will still be remembered in years to come. I have looked at YouTube and viewed the log books and really enjoyed your narration of them and would definitely like to purchase a book when it is completed.

I suppose I would be one of the younger members as I would only be three years of age when Pat founded the Club in 1945. I cannot remember exactly how I became a Member but suppose it would be via my Mum and her knowledge of what was going on in the area, as we only lived a short distance away on Rolleston Drive.

I remember very clearly dancing and miming to Tommy Steele singing 'The Only Man on the Island' at one of our concerts, also "The Fairy on the Christmas Tree' dressed in a tutu, possibly supplied by José, as she was the one connected with ballet. I always seemed to get the 'girlie' roles, possibly because I was quite petite as a youngster

I remember cooking our food on a fire down the fields and my bacon and eggs having all black bits on, nevertheless I still managed to eat it. We always had to make sure that the fire was well and truly out before we could leave. In summer we would be at the bottom of Mr and Mrs Stacey's garden, sitting on some type of boxes, in which we kept our papers and pencils, I think. I suppose these were one of Mr Stacey's acquisitions. Otherwise, we used their Front Room on a Tuesday evening for Club meetings and they also allowed us to use their lovely garden for Summer Concerts. They really were very kind.

I remained a member until the end and attended all the reunions over the years. At first we met up on a ten year basis at Nottingham Castle but then later we changed the venue to Arnot Hill Park, mostly in the Rose Garden, cutting down to a five year cycle, as we were all getting older and diminishing in numbers. I went to the last Get-Together, with my husband John, in June 2016. This was the last time that I saw the Log Books.

I really look forward to hearing from you when the Book is available and thank you so much for getting in touch.

Best wishes Betty Poole (nee Shaw)

Rosemary Neal

The most difficult member of the Sheredean Club to contact was Rosemary because she lives in Canada and even Pat could not give me her address but did suggest that her friend Betty Shaw may be able to get a message to her. I was delighted to receive an email message from Betty that she had told Rosemary about my request and that she would write to me with some memories of the Club. Sure enough, 4 days later I received this letter:-

Dear Michael,

I was a member of the Sheredean Club for a very short two years and the youngest member, I believe I was 11-13 years at the time. The Stacey's house was all of four houses up from ours and we all, on that side of the road had long gardens, so the garden shed meeting place seemed quite secluded.

There are two occasion that have stayed with me all these years:-

1 - The concerts we put on for the public to raise money for Dr Barnardo's, I believe, always seemed to me at that age, such a professional art of performing! Wendy played Fur Elise on the piano-both years and José, who was a dance teacher,

created a short piece for a group of us to perform. At that time I would have loved to be learning how to dance properly, with lessons-so I was thrilled to be on stage and dancing, even if I was doing a terrible job and forgetting steps. When José danced her solos, I thought she was quite wonderful.

2 - The second remembrance of that time was the weekend we hiked in the Derbyshire Dales-staying overnight in a Youth Hostel. With a not so nice remembrance of that weekend, we came across many dead rabbits from Myxomatosis.

Over the fifty years I have lived in Canada I have been a member of three, all women's groups, PEO, IODE and now with the WI.

I'm sure Sheredean Club and all its members was my initiation into Fund raising and helping others!

I hope you can read my writing - I am recovering from a dislocated shoulder.

I would very much like to purchase a copy of the book when published.

Sincerely Rosemary Trohill (Neal)

(I have written to Rosemary thanking her for this contribution and informing her that she will be able to obtain a copy of the book in Canada through Into Print, Michael Parkinson)

Sheredean Chapter 17

Pat and Derek Briggs
Written by Michael Parkinson

As YOUNGSTERS BOTH PAT AND Derek had singing lessons with Mrs Elsie Price at her home in Arnold and later at a studio in Nottingham. Mrs Price organised some of her pupils into a concert party and they performed at many venues around the area. One of the events was a 'Coronation Concert' on 23 May at Redhill County Secondary School which took place just before the coronation on 2 June 1953 of Queen Elizabeth II. Pat and Derek took part in this concert which was so popular that it was repeated in November that year.

Coronation

Concert

Presented by the pupils of
Mrs. T. H. Price L.L.C.M.

Saturday May 23rd, 1953

Concert Hall

Redhill County Secondary School
Arnold, Notts.

Commence 6.45 p.m.

Proceeds in aid of
The Nottingham Blind Institution and
Arnold Branch Old Age Pensioners' Ass.

Part 1

1. Pianoforte Solo   "Finlandia"   Bill Sutton

2. Operatic Medley   Phyllis Fell, Constance Forrest Irene Rudd, Pat Stacey, Harold Knighton,   Ron Sutton, Tom Hezseltine.

3. Acrobatic Dance   The Delroy Starlets
                                          (Stewart & Christine)

4. Sketch mime "The Tramp Scene"   The Midland
                                          Canoe Club

5. Vocal Duet   "Take the Sun"   Eileen Anthony
                                          Jean Williamson

6. Humorous Recitation   Effie Spick

7. "Rose Marie" (Excerpts)
                    Principals
Eileen Anthony, Phyllis Fell, Constance Forrest, Irene Rudd,
    Jean Williamson, Harold Knighton, Ron Sutton,
    Dancer Maureen Clayton, A.R.A.D. (Elem).
    Chorus of "Mounties" and Indian Dancers

At the Piano   -   .   .   Mrs. T. H. Price, L.L.C.M.

P2

Interval

Part 2

1. Part Song   "Nuns' Chorus"   *The Company*

2. Pianoforte Solo   "Glow Worm"   *Graham Parker*

3. Pianoforte Duet   *Maureen Bonser*
    Jane Vernon

4. Sketch   "Brave Men" ?   *The Midland Canoe Club*

5. A TRIBUTE TO OUR QUEEN

Britannia bids the Empire pay Homage in Song and Dance

Britannia   Effie Spick

India   *Joy Hallam*   Africa   *Madeline Fell*

New Zealand   *Margaret Hunter, Derek Briggs*

Australia   *Ivan Merriman, Eva Cooke, Audrey Banham.*

Canada   *Marian Warsop, Shirley Stanley.*

Ireland   *Errol Mason, Philip Clarke, Kenneth Richards, Shirley Mitchell, Dancer.*

Scotland   *Doreen Bradley, June Campion, Pat Frow,*

Wales   *Helga Mottishaw, Jose Sewell, Rose Twigg,*

England   *Eileen Anthony, Jean Williamson, Pauline Sully, Joan Clamp, Irene Brealey, Maureen Clayton, A.R.A.D. (Elem.) Dancer.*

Danse Militaire   Christine Preston

March of the Grenadiers   Pat Stacey and Chorus

Land of Hope and Glory   Phyllis Fell and Chorus

The Queen   P3

Mrs. Price gratefully thanks pupils and friends for their ...

The Coronation Concert page 1 - 2 - 3

Derek was born in Bristol on 3 October 1932 but the family had moved to Arnold by the time he went to primary school. He progressed to Nottingham High School where he became a prefect and played for the school rugby team. He was a member of the Combined Cadet Force, achieving the rank of Sergeant Major where he was top in rifle shooting and did two years National Service in the Royal Engineers at Aldershot.

In 1951 he attended Nottingham University studying geology, geography and physics and gained an honours degree in geology. This enabled him to get his first job with the National Coal Board in Sheffield where he worked as a field geologist in a team prospecting for coal. When he first moved to Sheffield Derek lodged with Mrs Peacock, at 183 Eccleshall Road. Mrs Peacock did not usually take in lodgers but she was the sister of Mrs Price, the teacher who had taught Pat and Derek singing when they lived in Arnold so made an exception because of the family connection. In January 1956 he was elected a Fellow of the Geology Society, London.

As described in Chapter 12 Pat Stacey became Mrs Pat Briggs when the couple were married on 7 September 1957. They set up their first home in a bungalow on Blackbrook Avenue, Lodge Moor, Sheffield where they later had two sons, Michael and Peter.

In 1959 Derek decided to take up teaching and worked at the Owler Lane Secondary Intermediate School in Sheffield before studying on a Post Graduate Certification in Education course at Sheffield University. When qualified, he taught geography and science at Marlcliffe Intermediate School in Sheffield from 1961 to 64. He moved to the Chaucer Comprehensive School where he taught geography, geology and science until 1967.

In 1942 Pat was a Brownie in the 1st Woodthorpe Pack and from 1945 to 50 was a guide in the 2nd Arnold Company and from 1950 to 55 was in the Arnold District Land Rangers whilst also helping with the guides. On moving to Sheffield in 1957 Pat helped with the Sharrow guides, Fulwood Guides in 58, the Deaf and Dumb Guides from 58 to 60 and was Captain of the 152nd Oughtibridge Guide Company section from 1960 to 66 as well as Camp Advisor at Sheffield North from 63 to 66.

A big change affected their lives in 1967 because Derek changed his job, moving to the Greatwood Camp Outdoor Centre which is situated in the Quantock Hills, Somerset. He ran the centre and worked with teachers to educate children in all aspects of local environment and natural history. He led them in adventurous activities including hill walking, orienteering and caving. This dream job change for Derek involved the family moving from Sheffield to a new bungalow at North Petherton.

On moving to Somerset, Pat continued her work with the Guide movement, she was Captain of 1st North Petherton Guides from 1968 to 1983 and District Commissioner of the Quantock District from 1972 to 1980. She gained a Campers Permit from 1952 to 55 and graduating to a Campers Licence in 1955. She was in charge of over 50 camps mostly with Derek (as a helper). Some camps were for Scouts and Guides including five indoor camps abroad. She obtained a good service award and quartermaster certificate in 1990 followed by awards for 30, 40 and 50 years service. She was awarded the Somerset County Standard Badge on her 80th birthday in 2014. Pat has also assisted at 3 camps to help Derek with scout camps in Belgium, Germany and Truro.

On 19 April 1978 Pat enrolled in the Trefoil Guild, a senior, non uniformed, Girl Guide group and received a Gold Award for her work on the Dark Horse Venture involving a trek to Peru in 1998. She is still a Trefoil member as I write in 2019.

Pat was also involved with the Rangers and Derek in the Scout Association where he became District Commissioner. Derek worked at the Greatwood Outdoor Centre for 17 years and then moved to Somerset County Council as an Advisory Teacher for environment, humanities and geology where he spent eleven years training teachers in those subjects. He had studied at Bristol Polytechnic in 1982/3 and gained a Certificate in Advanced Professional Studies in Environmental Education.

Pat and Derek were members of the North Petherton walking group from 2002 to 2015 and Pat arranged annual 'three night away holidays' involving booking accommodation, arranging finances and checking routes with Derek as the Walk Leader. She fell over and broke her wrist on a very wet day whilst out checking the route for a proposed holiday at Paignton and told me that, as a result, they did not use that walk.

Pat has been looking after the Children's Society Boxes at North Petherton Parish Church for over twenty five years. Her role is to collect the boxes up at the Christingle Service, count the money and pay it into the bank for the society. Derek accompanied her on two treks on behalf of the Society. In 2000 they went to Peru and walked and camped the Inca trail. The next year they trek camped in the Himalayas. They have given over thirty chat/slide show talks to different groups in Somerset giving donations of over £40 to the Children's Society after each presentation. In typical Pat style, she tells me that log books have been produced about these and the local guiding activities.

Pat, assisted by four different ladies over the years, jointly ran the 'Mary Poppins Playgroup' at the North Petherton Church rooms for 24 years. She has been a committee member of the North Petherton Community Centre for 40 years, starting before the centre was built and continuing with day to day running having special responsibilities for Brownies and Girl Guides.

Pat and Derek were presented with an Alfred Jewel Award Certificate on 18 July 1999 in recognition of exemplary and voluntary public service to the community of North Petherton. On 19 July 2005 they attended a Buckingham Palace Garden Party for services to the community.

Pat was awarded a certificate and badge for her work at the Campbell Room from the Scout Association in July 2010 and three years later an Award of Merit from that organisation. The Campbell Room provides self catering accommodation for groups in Somerset's Quantock Hills. Pat, Derek and the family have provided an additional building called 'The Briggs Cabin' named in memory of Derek and all the family who had worked on it for over 40 years. This was an extra cabin which the family built and equipped so that girls and boys could sleep in different rooms or as a craft room. Pat unveiled the sign in 2016 and son Michael still maintains the web site as I write in 2019. Pat and Derek have been members of the J Singers at Bridgwater for many years with Derek serving as Chairman for some time.

Derek, died aged 82 on 26 May 2015 and his colleagues of the J Singers sang 'You Raise Me Up' in what must have been an emotional part of the funeral service at North Petherton Church. I asked Pat to tell me how she and Derek originally became attached to each other and was surprised to receive these very personal snippets of information:-

Saturday 9 September 1950 - We dance together for the first time.

Friday 15 September 1950 - Hold hands.

Sunday 17 September 1950 - Spend the evening together at 66 Sandfield Road.

Sunday 12 November 1950 - First kiss.

Sunday 19 November 1950 - Express our love for each other.

Thursday 4 January 1951 - Dance at the Astoria Ballroom, Nottingham.

Sunday 21 January 1951 - Walk to Mapperley and Redhill.

Sunday 18 March 1951 - Bike cleaning in shed and tea at 66 Sandfield Road.

I expressed surprise that Pat could provide such detailed intimate memories after all those years and she replied 'I found a piece of paper with it all on whilst looking through Dereks belongings' she added mischievously 'there was a lot more very sensitive information that I will not tell you about'.

Pat still takes part in many activities in North Petherton and Bridgwater and I am proud to be involved with writing the story of the Sheredean Club and her life with Derek.

Pat and Derek visiting an outbuilding at Fosters nursery in 1997

Sheredean Chapter 18

Ovaltine story 1865 to 2019
Written by Michael Parkinson

THE OVALTINE STORY STARTED IN 1865 when Dr George Wander a Swiss Chemist based in Bern established the high nutritional value of barley malt. He then began to manufacture malt extract and launched the food drink 'Ovolmaltine'. This quickly became a success and was recommended by doctors as a health product. In the early years small quantities of Ovolmaltine and assorted pharmaceutical preparations were imported to Britain from Switzerland. In 1900 his son Albert took over the business and in 1909, a company named A. Wander Ltd, was set up to sell and later manufacture Ovaltine, as it was called in Britain. In 1913 a small factory was opened at Kings Langley in Hertfordshire, with an original work force of 13 people.

In 1925 Wander opened a prestigious head office at Queen's Gate in London and Mr Harry Hague was appointed Managing Director with a mandate to develop the company which he did with great success. The business expanded rapidly and by 1930 the factory had been extended and was built up to its maximum capacity.

Coal for the factory was brought by barge along the Grand Union Canal from Warwickshire collieries. Each barge and the butty boat that it towed carried 42 tons of coal and there was a fleet of barges, or narrow boats as they are now known, in constant use. In 1925 Wander decided to introduce its own boats and in January of the next year the first pair, motor Albert and the butty, Georgette, entered service (the motor boat usually had a male name and the butty a female name). By 1954 the fleet was reduced to 3 pairs as contractors were increasingly delivering coal by road. Eventually the company switched from coal to oil and the obsolete barges were sold off by Wander Ltd and some were broken up.

In December 1988 the remains of narrow boat 'Albert' were noticed lying at the bottom of a canal near Nottingham. Chris Collins and Tim Woodbridge saved the craft and re-built it before it was re-launched on the Grand Union Canal in 1990. The name 'Albert' was retained in honour of Albert Wander.

The refurbished narrow boat

The first Ovaltine press advertisement appeared in 1913, prepared by advertising agents Saward Baker & Co Ltd. In 1920 they introduced Horace Bury to Wander and over the next 40 years he created over 2000 press and magazine advertisements. This figure was so high because the company policy was 'never to repeat an advertisement in more than one journal'. The most famous marketing feature was the Radio Luxembourg Ovaltineys Show which was launched on Sunday 23 December 1934 and was broadcast every Sunday. The 'League of Ovaltineys' was started in 1935, children applied for membership using forms attached to Ovaltine packaging, and by 1939 had over 5 million members. As described in chapter 1, eight year old Pat Stacey and a few of her friends were members in 1941. Pat was issued with 'The official rule book' and 78 years later has sent it to me so that it can be included here.

OFFICIAL RULE BOOK of
The League of Ovaltineys

WARNING! This book is strictly private. It contains confidential rules and secrets that are intended for members of The League of Ovaltineys only. If lost, the finder is requested to return it, WITHOUT OPENING, to the owner whose name is on the back cover.

Headquarters of
The League of Ovaltineys
184 Queen's Gate, London S.W.7.

Dear Friend,

I am very glad to welcome you into the League of Ovaltineys. I am sure that you will have lots of fun and will make a great many jolly friends among the Ovaltineys.

Do you know that this great League of ours is now over five years old? It has many thousands of members all over the British Isles, throughout the Empire and in other parts of the world. Doesn't it make you feel proud to belong to such an important League?

Now that you are a member, I am sending you your Official Rule Book. Look first at the opposite page and study our seven Golden Rules. Sign your name at the bottom as a promise that you will live up to them and be a loyal Ovaltiney.

After that, pin your badge firmly on your jacket or blouse - on the left side, over your heart - and everyone will know that you are a real, full-fledged Ovaltiney. Later on you will want to become an Officer of our League and earn the shining Silver Star and the Gold Bar. You can read all about these badges of high rank on pages 6 and 7.

And remember - this book is absolutely secret. Print your name clearly in the blank space on the back cover to show it belongs to you, and keep the book in some safe, private place so that it can't possibly get lost.

Your friend,

The Chief Ovaltiney

The 7 GOLDEN RULES
of the League of Ovaltineys

Every member is expected to live up to our 7 Golden Rules. They are very important, so read them carefully in private where you won't be disturbed. Then sign your name at the bottom of the page.

I PROMISE to do the things my parents tell me to—because they know what's best for me and I want them to be proud of me.

I PROMISE to get plenty of exercise, indoors and out—because exercise and fresh air help to keep me always healthy, strong and vigorous.

I PROMISE to study hard at school—because I want to have a good, keen mind, and I also promise to avoid danger by looking in every direction before crossing roads.

I PROMISE to get lots of good sound sleep—because every growing girl and boy needs plenty of sleep at night in order to do their best at school next day.

I PROMISE to eat the things my Mother wants me to—like vegetables and fruit—because she knows what's good for me

I PROMISE to drink Ovaltine regularly every day—so I can be healthy, happy and full of vim like all true Ovaltineys.

I PROMISE to be a loyal member of The League of Ovaltineys by learning all of the rules by heart and keeping them faithfully—by never telling the official secrets to anyone who is not a member—and by helping other people in every way I can.

I hereby agree to keep these promises to the best of my ability.

Signed: _Patricia Ann Stacey_

(Write your name right here on this line)

SECRET SIGNS *and* SIGNALS
OF THE LEAGUE

NOW we come to the official secret signs and signals that only members of the League of Ovaltineys can know and use.

Remember that these are *absolutely confidential* and should *never* be revealed to anyone who is not a member. Study each one carefully and practise it in the mirror until you can do it as quick as a flash.

CHUCKLE !

SECRET PASSWORD

Sometimes outsiders may pretend that they are Ovaltineys so as to discover our secrets. Whenever you want to find out for sure whether anyone is a member of the League, ask him to give the password to prove it.

You say : Give the password.

He should answer : CHUCKLE

If he cannot give the password, he is an impostor and doesn't belong to the League at all.

SECRET DOOR KNOCK

This is the secret door knock of the League of Ovaltineys : 4 slow knocks followed by 4 quick knocks. You do it like this : 1-2-3-4 (pause) 1234. You use this secret knock to gain admittance to secret meetings—or whenever you want someone inside to know that there is an Ovaltiney waiting to get in.

2

SECRET SIGNS AND SIGNALS (continued)

OFFICIAL WHISTLE

The official whistle of the League is *four* sharp notes. Use it when you are calling for other members, or if you want to attract their attention when outsiders are present who might notice the regular wig-wag signs.

SECRET HIGH-SIGN

The high-sign is a sort of *secret greeting* you give fellow members instead of just saying "hello" as you do to ordinary people. *To give the* high-sign, place the first finger of each hand just in front of each ear. Your thumb and all your other fingers should be curled up in your hand. The picture shows you how to do it. Practise it in front of a mirror a few times and you'll find it perfectly easy.

SECRET COUNTER SIGN

The counter-sign is the *answer* to the high-sign. If a friend salutes you with the high-sign, you must give him the counter-sign. This is very easy. Just put your finger tips together, the *back* of the right hand touching the *front* of the left hand—and hold them up in front of your chin. The picture shows you how to do this.

3

SECRET WIG-WAG SIGNS

This is a sort of secret "deaf-and-dumb" sign language—done with the hands so that you can say things to other members silently without speaking a word

WIG-WAG SIGN No. 1

When you hook your *little fingers* together it means: "Look out! Danger! Outsiders are trying to discover our Ovaltiney secrets."

"Look out! Danger! Outsiders are trying to discover our Ovaltiney secrets."

"I have an important secret message that I want to give you in private."

WIG-WAG SIGN No. 2

When you hook your *thumbs* together, it means: "I have an important secret message that I want to give you in private."

WIG-WAG SIGN No. 3

When you put your *right fist* on top of your *left fist* it means: "Let's hurry home; it's 'Ovaltine' time."

NOTE—You will find all the wig-wag signs very useful when Ovaltiney matters are being discussed and a non-member approaches.

"Let's hurry home; it's 'Ovaltine' time!"

4

THE OVALTINEYS' CERTIFICATE OF MERIT

When an Ovaltiney has done something especially fine—something brave or helpful or clever—he is presented with a Certificate of Merit. The picture above shows you what this looks like. A silken cord is threaded through the top so that it can be hung on the wall where people can admire it.

Naturally, every Ovaltiney is keen to win this great honour. So if you have done something which your father and mother, or your teacher or friends, admire write and tell the Chief Ovaltiney about it. If he thinks it worthy, your name will be entered on the Ovaltineys' Roll of Honour, and you will be awarded the Ovaltineys' Certificate of Merit

HOW TO BECOME A
SILVER STAR MEMBER

1. Tell three friends about the League and get them to join. Ask them all to give you a paper disc from inside the lid of a tin of 'Ovaltine.'

2. Fill in the pink form supplied and post with the three paper discs to The Chief Ovaltiney, 184, Queen's Gate, London, S.W.7.

3. In a few days the postman will bring you a beautiful Silver Star. And your three friends will receive their bronze members' badges and the Official Rule Book.

ONCE you are a member of the League of Ovaltineys, you can start to work for your Silver Star badge. This is the badge of an Officer of the League. It shows that you are in a position of authority and belong to the Inner Circle of the League. New members will look to you for advice and instruction. You can organise meetings or form your own particular section of the League.

Winning your Silver Star is as simple as A-B-C. Read the instructions under the pictures on this page and you will learn exactly what to do.

Then start right away to tell your friends about the League. Tell them of all the exciting things we do, and how they can never understand our secret high-signs and signals until they become members themselves. And tell them, too, how scrumptious 'Ovaltine' is and how it makes boys and girls healthy and strong and gives them lots of energy for work and play.

6

THE GOLD BAR FOR SILVER STAR MEMBERS

HERE'S THE WAY TO GET IT!

THE supreme goal of every Ovaltiney is the Gold Bar. This is the highest honour the League can offer, and it can only be won by Silver Star members.

To win the Gold Bar you must enrol *three more members* for the League. Talk to your friends ; tell them of all the fun that Ovaltineys have and of the good the League is doing. They will soon be keen to join. Ask them all to bring you a paper slip or disc from inside a tin of 'Ovaltine.' Fill in their names and addresses—and, of course, your *own* name and address— on the green form enclosed and post it, together with the three discs, to the Chief Ovaltiney.

In a few days your friends will receive their Bronze Badges and Rule Books, and *you* will receive the greatest honour of all, the Ovaltiney Gold Bar. Remember, Gold Bar members are captains and are very important Ovaltineys indeed.

7

Take good care of this book. It contains important private information. If this book is lost, the finder is requested to return it to the owner (name below) WITHOUT OPENING.

This Certifies That PAT STACEY, 66 SANDFIELD RD,

is a fully fledged member of the League of Ovaltineys.

The official book pages 1 to 12

The name Ovaltineys did not derive directly from the product but a clever play on words. In the early 1930s a stage show was originated and presented by Harry Hemsley near the Oval in South London. (close to the famous cricket ground). He coined the phrase 'Oval tinies' because of the location and the fact that the performers were small children. In the 1980s a new team of young Ovaltineys were formed and their first long playing record reached the top twenty. Here is the list of songs on that disc, I am sure they revive nostalgic memories to many people.

1   We are the Ovaltineys
2   Happy Days are Here Again
3   Painting the Clouds with Sunshine
4   On the Sunny Side of the Street
5   Tip-toe through the Tulips with Me
6   Shine on Harvest Moon
7   The Umbrella Man
8   Lets all sing like the birdies sing
9   On the Good Ship Lollipop
10 An Apple for the Teacher
11 Rolling Along
12 The Teddy Bears' Picnic
13 Who's Afraid of the Big Bad Wolf
14 Heigh-ho (from the film Snow White)
15 Winter Wonderland
16 The Lambeth Walk
17 Wish me Luck as you wave me Goodbye
18 The Ovaltineys say Goodbye

From the humble start in 1913 the number of employees at the factory rose to 1400 in 1950 before automation reduced the figure to about 350 in 1990 prior to the closure in 2002. In addition to Ovaltine, Options Hot Chocolate was made. The company became the biggest liquid malt extract producer in the world, not only is it used in Ovaltine but the inside of Maltesers and many other well known biscuits and sweets.

In 1967 Wander Ltd merged with a Swiss firm Sandoz Ltd. After this, business remained the same for Wander, but in 1996 Sandoz merged with CIBA (a Swiss Chemical Company) and the Ovaltine factory name had to change from Wander to Novartis.

In October 2002 the Ovaltine part of the business was acquired by the Twinings Group of Associated British Foods. They closed the factory at Kings Langley and transferred all of the production to Wander AG at Neuenegg, near Bern, Switzerland. As I write in 2019, Ovaltine products are still supplied to Britain from that factory in Switzerland and there are three more factories at Shanghai, Melbourne and Bangkok, in addition a variety of Ovaltine products are manufactured and marketed by Nestlé in America.

Whilst researching for this book, in March 2019, I visited Kings Langley and walked up Egg Farm Lane in order to visit the old Egg Farm buildings. I was greeted by Mr Rob Armstrong, the Group Head of Communications and Marketing of Renewable Energy Solutions (RES) who imparted very interesting information. I learned that in 1929 A Wander Ltd purchased local farms so that they could produce some of the ingredients used in the manufacture of Ovaltine, and one of them was the Egg Farm. They constructed the farm buildings in a large horseshoe shape with the arc of the curve facing south and large windows designed to attract solar heat. The buildings housed the poultry farm which reared thousands of chicks before they were placed outside in hen houses with access outside so the hens were outdoors for some of the time. Eggs were gathered by workers and placed into large baskets before being conveyed to the factory.

The farm was closed in the 1960s and lay derelict until 2002 when RES took it over. Rob told me that initially men with large shovels had to remove loads of chicken excrement before the buildings were adapted, and some new construction added for the office headquarters of RES. I was surprised to learn that RES harness solar power but in a more sophisticated way than Wander Ltd used it for the poultry farm many years ago. They have a huge array of solar panels which, in summer, heat water to about 40 degrees centigrade.

This is stored in a huge underground insulated container and, in winter, is used to heat the office complex. Conversely, they have made a borehole which uses cold water (about 12 degrees centigrade) from 75 metres underground to pump through the pipes to keep the offices cool in summer.

Briefly, RES is a private company established in the 1980s within the UK's Sir Robert McAlpine engineering and construction group.

Well and dovecote at the egg farm, preserved by RES

Collectors at the egg farm perhaps get better pic when I take video back

Later that day I walked along Station Road, at Kings Langley, to the site of the old Ovaltine factory, now called Ovaltine Court. Although the factory building appears to be still intact, in fact, only the facade remains with Ovaltine, in huge letters, and the famous Dairy Maid, featured prominently. Behind the facade, impressive living accommodation replaces what was once the factory and extends to the bank of the Grand Union Canal. This was once the noisy and dirty coal unloading wharf but is now an area of tranquil beauty. The surrounding area includes a large play area and extensive private housing with road names like Ovaltine Drive, Wander Wharf and Grand Union Way.

The top of the 4 storey high facade

In compiling this chapter I have used information kindly supplied by:- Kings Langley Local History & Museum Society, Novartis Video 'The Ovaltine Story', Renewable Energy Systems, Associated British Foods (ABF) and Wander AG Neuenegg, Switzerland. I am grateful for help given to me by Hertfordshire County Libraries.

Sheredean Chapter 19

Dr Barnardo's Homes
Written by Michael Parkinson

THE SHEREDEAN CLUB DONATED MONEY to Dr Barnardo's Homes between 1947 and 1961 and there are many references to that organisation in this book. I am particularly impressed of how good they were at sending receipts and letters of thanks when donations were made. Chapter 8 includes a description of the Club visiting the Barnardo's Home at Holbrook in Derbyshire. Whilst chapter 14 includes an emotional account of how the story began. Many years have elapsed since then so I approached Barnardo's, and was given permission to include the up to date Dr Barnardo's story in my book, here it is:-

Thomas John Barnardo was born in Dublin, Ireland, in 1845. As a young man he moved to London to train as a doctor. When he arrived, he was shocked to find children living in terrible conditions, with no access to education. Poverty and disease were so widespread that one in five children died before their fifth birthday. When a cholera epidemic swept through the East End, leaving 3000 people dead and many orphaned children, the young Barnardo felt an urgent need to help. His first step, in 1867, was to set up a 'ragged school' where children could get a free basic education. One evening a boy at the mission, Jim Jarvis, took Barnardo around the East End, showing him children sleeping on roofs and in gutters. What he saw affected him so deeply he decided to abandon his medical training and devote himself to helping children living in poverty.

In 1870, Barnardo opened his first home for boys. As well as putting a roof over their heads, the home trained the boys in carpentry, metalwork and shoemaking, and found apprenticeships for them. To begin with, there was a limit to the number of boys who could stay there. But when an 11-year-old boy was found dead, of malnutrition and exposure, two days after being told the shelter was full, Barnardo vowed never to turn away another child.

Barnardo's work was radical. The Victorians saw poverty as shameful, and the result of laziness or vice. But Barnardo refused to discriminate between the 'deserving' and 'undeserving' poor. He accepted all children, including black and disabled children, and those born outside marriage. Barnardo believed that every child deserved the best possible start in life, whatever their background. This philosophy still guides the charity today.

In 1873 Barnardo married Syrie Louise Elmslie, who was to play an important role in the development of the charity. As a wedding present, they were given a lease on a 60 acre site in Barkingside, east London, where the couple opened a home for girls. Syrie was especially keen to support girls who had been driven to prostitution. Protecting children from sexual exploitation continues to be an important part of their work today. The Barnardos were early adopters of the 'cottage homes' model. They believed that children could be best supported if they were living in small, 'family style groups' looked after by a house 'mother'. By 1900 the Barkingside 'garden village' had 65 cottages, a school, a hospital and a church, and provided a home and training to 1500 girls.

Thomas Barnardo at his desk

Barnardo went on to found many more children's homes. By the time he died on 19th September 1905, the charity had 96 homes caring for more than 8,500 vulnerable children. This included children with physical and learning difficulties. Barnardo's experience of caring for his daughter Marjorie, who had Down's syndrome, strongly influenced his approach to the care of children with disabilities.

Although he was famous for his children's homes, Barnardo believed that ideally a child should grow up in a family setting. As early as 1887 he introduced the practice of 'boarding out' children to host families, an early form of fostering. This wasn't a popular idea in Victorian England, but Barnardo was determined to give children the best possible futures. By 1905 more than 4000 children were boarded out. This paved the way for pioneering work in foster care and adoption in the twentieth century.

Barnardo's admit that they were one of many children's charities that sent some children to start a new life in Australia or Canada from the late nineteenth century to the 1960s. This was a popular policy, supported by the British government, who believed that the children would benefit from opportunities they wouldn't have in the UK. They now know that however well intentioned, it was a deeply misguided policy. The last Barnardo's child to be migrated was in 1967, to Australia. In 2010 the British government formally apologised for the UK's role in sending more than 130,000 child migrants to former colonies.

World War II was a turning point in Barnardo's development, and in the history of childcare in the UK. The disruption brought by war highlighted the harmful effect that separation from their families had on children. As a result, Barnardo's began to work more closely with families. For example, they offered financial aid to families when the breadwinner couldn't work because of illness or accident. By the end of the 1950s almost a quarter of the work involved helping children stay with their own families.

The 1960s were a time of radical social change: single parenthood was more acceptable, contraception more widely available (leading to fewer unwanted pregnancies) and a growing welfare system meant that fewer families needed to put their children into care. As well as their decision to work more with families, the need for children's homes was decreasing, so they began to focus less on residential services. Instead, developed their work with disabled children and children with emotional and behavioural difficulties.

In the 1970s Barnardo's continued to expand fostering adoption services and created family centres to support families in deprived areas. The last children's home closed in 1989. In the 1980s and 1990s they developed new ways of working with children and young people, including pioneering work supporting survivors of child sexual abuse and children affected by HIV and Aids.

One of their biggest supporters at this time was the late Diana, Princess of Wales, who was President of Barnardo's from 1984 to 1996. Her caring approach to supporting vulnerable children and young people reflected Barnardo's methods of working.

Princess Diana on the left

Today, Barnardo's support and protect children and young people facing a wide range of issues, from drug misuse to disability, from sexual abuse to domestic violence. But one thing has never changed, like founder, Thomas Barnardo, they believe that with the right help, children can change their lives and achieve their potential. Over 150 years ago, Barnardo promised to support those children in need of help, regardless of their circumstances, gender, race, disability or behaviour. As I write in 2019, Barnardo's continue to honour that promise.

We've come a long way since our founder, Thomas Barnardo set up a 'ragged school' to help disadvantaged children in 1867. Now we're helping hundreds of thousands of children, young people, parents and carers across the UK. We don't abandon children because of who they are or what they've done. We listen to them, fight for their rights and do whatever it takes to protect and support them because we believe that all children have the right to a happy and healthy life. At a time when more young people need specialist help with complex issues like sexual abuse, mental health problems and serious violence, our work is more vital than ever. Times have changed and we've changed with them, but our belief in the potential of every child remains. Because this is who we are.

You can see more about Barnardo's (as it is now known) on their web site www.barnardos.org this includes case studies, opportunities to make donations, and more interesting information.

Sheredean Chapter 20

The Youth Hostel Association (YHA)
Written by Michael Parkinson

PAT STACEY AND DEREK BRIGGS were both junior members of the YHA and had enjoyed many visits to Youth Hostels before graduating to senior membership later on. When they were married in 1957, they continued to stay at Youth Hostels either as a couple or as organisers of various youth groups. Pat has given me a comprehensive list with the year and names of places where they have stayed between 1955 and 2012. I hope that some who read this chapter will recognise some of the hostels and may have memories of staying in them.

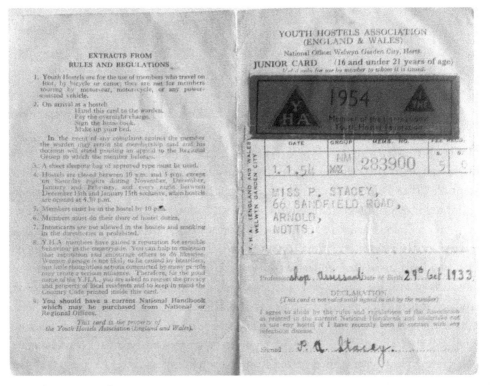

Pat's YHA card

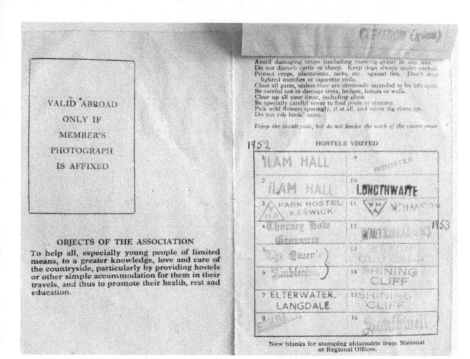

OBJECTS OF THE ASSOCIATION

To help all, especially young people of limited means, to a greater knowledge, love and care of the countryside, particularly by providing hostels or other simple accommodation for them in their travels, and thus to promote their health, rest and education.

Avoid damaging crops (including mowing-grass) in any way.
Do not disturb cattle or sheep. Keep dogs always under control.
Protect crops, plantations, ricks, etc. against fire. Don't drop lighted matches or cigarette ends.
Close all gates, unless they are obviously intended to be left open.
Be careful not to damage trees, hedges, fences or walls.
Clear up all your litter, including glass.
Be specially careful never to foul pools or streams.
Pick wild flowers sparingly, if at all, and never dig them up.
Do not rob birds' nests.

Enjoy the countryside, but do not hinder the work of the countryman

1952 · HOSTELS VISITED

1 ILAM HALL	9 MINISTER
2 ILAM HALL	10 LONGTHWAITE
3 PARK HOSTEL KESWICK	11 KESWICK
4 Thorney How Grasmere	12 WHIT... 1953
5 The Queen's	13
6 Ambleside	14 SHINING CLIFF
7 ELTERWATER, LANGDALE	15 SHINING CLIFF
8	16

New blanks for stamping obtainable from National or Regional Offices.

Inside of the card

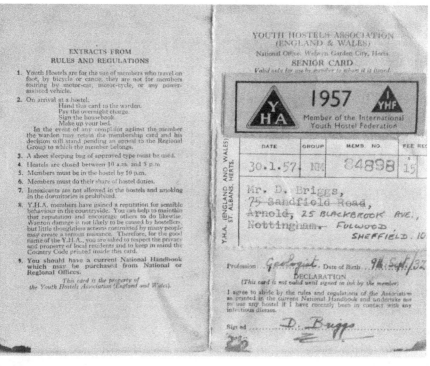

EXTRACTS FROM RULES AND REGULATIONS

1. Youth Hostels are for the use of members who travel on foot, by bicycle or canoe, they are not for members touring by motor-car, motor-cycle, or any power-assisted vehicle.

2. On arrival at a hostel.
   Hand this card to the warden.
   Pay the overnight charge.
   Sign the housebook.
   Make up your bed.
   In the event of any complaint against the member the warden may retain the membership card and his decision will stand pending an appeal to the Regional Group to which the member belongs.

3. A sheet sleeping bag of approved type must be used.

4. Hostels are closed between 10 a.m. and 5 p.m.

5. Members must be in the hostel by 10 p.m.

6. Members must do their share of hostel duties.

7. Intoxicants are not allowed in the hostels and smoking in the dormitories is prohibited.

8. Y.H.A. members have gained a reputation for sensible behaviour in the countryside. You can help to maintain that reputation and encourage others to do likewise. Wanton damage is not likely to be caused by hostellers, but little thoughtless actions committed by many people may create a serious nuisance. Therefore, for the good name of the Y.H.A., you are asked to respect the privacy and property of local residents and to keep in mind the Country Code printed inside this card.

9. You should have a current National Handbook which may be purchased from National or Regional Offices.

   This card is the property of the Youth Hostels Association (England and Wales).

YOUTH HOSTELS ASSOCIATION
(ENGLAND & WALES)
National Office, Welwyn Garden City, Herts.

SENIOR CARD
Valid only for use by member to whom it is issued.

Y H A · **1957** · I YHF
Member of the International Youth Hostel Federation

Y.H.A. (ENGLAND AND WALES) ST. ALBANS, HERTS.

DATE	GROUP	MEMB. NO.	FEE REC
30.1.57	NM	84898	15

Mr. D. Briggs,
75 Sandfield Road,
Arnold, 25 BLACKBROOK AVE.,
Nottingham. FULWOOD
SHEFFIELD. 10

Profession ...Geologist... Date of Birth ...9th. Sept./32

DECLARATION
(This card is not valid until signed in ink by the member)

I agree to abide by the rules and regulations of the Association as printed in the current National Handbook and undertake not to use any hostel if I have recently been in contact with any infectious disease.

Signed ....D. Briggs..........

Derek's YHA card

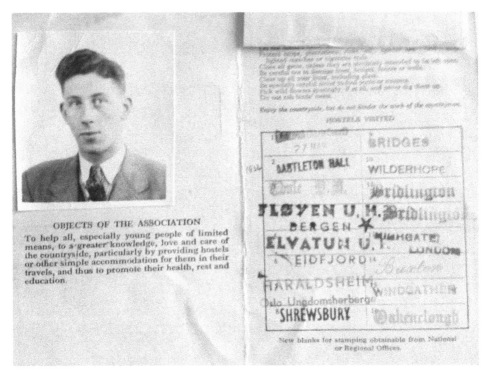

Inside of the card

1955

    Elton Old Hall

    Hartington

    Ilam Hall (Three visits in the year)

    Southwell

    Bridlington (Two visits in the year)

    Highgate, London

1956

    Whissendine (Two visits this year)

    Loddington

    Buxton

    Windgather

    Oakenclough

    Rudyard Lake (Two visits this year)

    Leam Hall (Two visits in the year)

    Foxhill, Colwyn Bay (Two visits this year)

    EBIW Farm, Rowen

    Oaklands

Capel Cunia
Snowdon, Ranger (Bryd ddu)
Gorad-y-Gyt, Bangor
Arnside (Two visits this year)
Ravenstor

1957
Hutton (Three visits this year)
Cheddar
Bristol
Chepstow
St Briavels Castle
Welsh Bicknor, Ross-on-Wye
Ilam Hall
Leam Hall

1958
Ambleside
High Close, Loughbrigg
Thorney How, Grasmere
Keswick
Honister House
Eskdale
Holly How, Coniston

1959
Ravenstor
Elton Old Hall

1960
Leam Hall

1961
Ravenstor

1962
Leam Hall
Rudyard Lake
White House, Scarborough

1965
Windgather

1972
Tavistock
Maypool
Holford, Bridgwater (Two visits this year)

Crickhowell

House Mitcheldean

1973

King George V1 Memorial, London

1982

Llanddeusant (Two visits this year)

1984

Westerdale Hall (Two visits this year)

1988

King George V1 Memorial, London (Two visits this year)

Holford, Bridgwater (Two visits this year)

1999

Llanberis

2010

Sherwood Forest (Three visits this year)

2012

Bristol (Three visits this year, with Guides)

Eyam (Two visits this year)

It is obvious from the hostels visited by Pat and Derek that YHA accepted adult as well as youth members. I had a personal reason to find out about this in 2016.

I had arranged to put 14 performances of my Billy Fury Dance Show on at the Shaw Theatre which is situated next to the British Library on Euston Road in London. I investigated various hotels until a friend suggested trying the YHA at St Pancras. My initial reaction was to say, 'We could not stay there because we are not youngsters' My friend told me that they do in fact accept adults at Youth Hostels. I went to the YHA situated at 79/81 Euston Road, London and booked Joan and myself in for 14 nights in an en suite room situated on the 4th floor with extensive views. It was cheap and cheerful, the breakfast was good and we enjoyed speaking to the other residents, many from abroad. The location was ideal for our needs being close to St Pancras Station and the Shaw Theatre.

Whilst compiling this book, in 2019, I visited the hostel and the duty manageress told me that it is purpose built with 48 rooms and 200 beds with occupancy of 93% capacity over the last year so it is very well used.

YHA London St Pancras

One of over 150 Youth Hostels
throughout England & Wales.

Accommodation

Private rooms and shared dormitory
accommodation available
Most rooms with en-suite facilities

·

Café bar

Fully licensed and serving tasty meals
throughout the day, free WiFi

·

Fully equipped conference facilities

·

Discounted attraction and travel tickets available

·

One of the UK's top 50 charities

Creating unique opportunities for young people
throughout England & Wales

Pop in or call us on 0845 371 9344
stpancras@yha.org.uk
www.yha.org.uk

YHA map on the wall at St Pancras

The very first Youth Hostel was opened in Germany in 1909 by school teacher Richard Schirrmann. Twenty years later, following a trip to Germany, a small group of pioneers opened Britain's first Youth Hostel. The national organisation was established the following year and, by Easter 1931, 11 hostels were open.

YHA is a child of the Great Depression. The welfare of Britain's growing urban population was a serious concern in the early 20th century. YHA's offer of affordable accommodation was an antidote to the poor air quality, cramped housing and harsh conditions of inner city life. It gave young working people an unprecedented opportunity to spend leisure time in fresh air and open countryside, on a scale only previously possible for the wealthy.

During the Second World War the number of YHA members doubled. By the 80s, the needs of the modern-day traveller were changing and YHA went through significant development in this era: introducing smaller, private rooms, improving facilities and adopting a professional management structure.

Since 2011 the YHA have invested over £37 million in their hostels. They have refurbished treasured historic buildings, improved facilities network-wide and acquired new properties to add more choice to visitors. As I write in 2019 the YHA provides great value accommodation in towns and cities, as well as in the countryside and on the coast. They offer premium and family en-suite rooms as well as dorm rooms, They have made many changes over the years but have tried to stay true to their core mission which is:-

To inspire all, especially young people, to broaden their horizons, gaining knowledge and independence through new experiences of adventure and discovery.

Pat introduced many girls to the YHA through the Sheredean Club, Girl Guides and Rangers. Derek introduced many youngsters to the YHA through his voluntary work with the Boy scouts and in his work at the Greatwood Outdoor Centre in Somerset. They took advantage of the International Federation to visit hostels abroad where there are hostels in many countries.

The YHA has a charitable fund that supports 'Breaks for Kids'. They believe that every young person should have the opportunity to travel to new places and discover new environments away from home with their friends. They know from long involvement how valuable, how eye-opening, and in some cases, how life changing these experiences can be. They help children to grow in confidence, to increase self-awareness and to achieve a sense of belonging.

Sheredean Postscript

My YouTube channel name Michael notthatone Parkinson
Written by Michael Parkinson

THANK YOU FOR READING THIS book, whilst I am stated to be the author I have actually copy typed (with just a few comments from me) Chapters 2 to 15 which of course had been originally written by the members of the Sheredean Club between 1945 and 1960.

In Chapter one I explained that my reaction to reading the Sheredean Log Books was to make and load 15 videos to YouTube with me reading the text accompanied by video so that the viewer can hear the words and see exactly how the text was written. As the writing was done directly into the Log Books there was no opportunity to cancel and start again as writers are able to do today. I realise that many people do not have access to YouTube but for those that do I list the titles:-

Name of YouTube video		Comment
Sheredean Girls Story	Introduction	Including pre decimal money explanation
Sheredean Girls Story	Part 1	From start to 1949
"	2	From 1950 to Dr B letter 23 Jan51
"	3	Results year 1950 to pics camping 51
"	4	Mystery outing to end of 1952
"	5	Oxton camp to letter Dr B all boys home
"	6	Start, pic Janet Pat etc 8 Sep ends Meresia
"	7	Start, walk Gedling Lane 54 ends Dunwich
"	8	Start, Dunwich camp end receipt 11 Jan 55
"	9	Start, 1955 ends pictures of camping
"	10	Starts, Janet left the club ends camping
"	11	Starts, in 1956 ends Dr B pictures
"	12	Starts, Daily Sketch ends Dr B 13 Jan 59
"	13	Starts, 1959 ends Dr B letter 6 Jan 1960
"	14	Starts, 1960 ends Pat/Derek wedding photo

I have loaded a video to YouTube which includes on screen words and sound of the chorus which opened the Ovaltineys Radio Luxembourg show for many years. This has the title 'Ovaltineys to Sheredean Girls Club 1941 to 1960'.

Michael Parkinson

Other Titles from Michael Parkinson

Michael describes how he wrote a script and produced shows with dancers performing routines and narrators telling the Billy Fury story. There is a biography of Britain's first Rock 'n' Roll Star. He tells background stories about some of his YouTube videos including Saara Aalto of X Factor and Ice Dancing fame. He walked the Thames Path in short sections spanning three years with descriptions of each section. There is an account of Judith Durham when she performed an emotional farewell concert with the Seekers at Nottingham. Disneyland Paris and the Thursford Christmas Spectacular precede autobiographical chapters about childhood, National Service and adult life. The Gardener and the Alzheimers lady is amongst many unusual but true stories in the 39 chapters covering a variety of subjects.

ISBN 978-1-78222-588-1

Lightning Source UK Ltd.
Milton Keynes UK
UKHW020154260619
345026UK00002B/4/P